# AN UNBROKEN CIRCLE

D0869832

# THE NEGRO SPEAKS OF RIVERS

I've known rivers:
I've known rivers ancient as the world and older than the flow
of human blood in human veins.

My soul has grown deep like the rivers.

I bathed in the Euphrates when dawns were young.
I built my hut near the Congo and it lulled me to sleep.
I looked upon the Nile and raised the pyramids above it.
I heard the singing of the Mississippi when Abe Lincoln went
down to New Orleans, and I've seen its muddy bosom turn
all golden in the sunset.

I've known rivers:
Ancient, dusky rivers.

My soul has grown deep like the rivers.

*Langston Hughes*

# AN UNBROKEN CIRCLE

## LINKING ANCIENT AFRICAN CHRISTIANITY
## TO THE AFRICAN-AMERICAN EXPERIENCE

## FATHER PAISIUS ALTSCHUL
### EDITOR

## BROTHERHOOD OF ST. MOSES THE BLACK
### ST. LOUIS, MISSOURI · 1997

Grateful acknowledgment is made to the Lilly Endowment, Indianapolis, Indiana, for its financial support of this project.

"The Negro Speaks of Rivers," from COLLECTED POEMS by Langston Hughes, Copyright © 1994 by the Estate of Langston Hughes. Reprinted by permission of Alfred A. Knopf Inc.

FRONT COVER: Icon of St. Moses the Black by Archimandrite Cyprian, Holy Trinity Monastery, Jordanville, New York.

BACK COVER: The icon of St. Moses the Black was painted expressly for this publication by Nun Catherine of the Liturgical Arts Association of the Black Madonna.

Printed in the United States of America.

Published by the Brotherhood of St. Moses the Black
P.O. Box 63377
St. Louis, MO 63163

LIBRARY OF CONGRESS CATALOGING-IN-PUBLICATION DATA

An unbroken circle : linking ancient African Christianity to the
    African-American experience / Paisius Altschul, editor.
        p.   cm.
    Essays derived from lectures and testimonies presented at the
Ancient Christianity and African-America Conferences, held in
Kansas City, Mo. and Indianapolis, Ind.
    Includes bibliographical references.
    ISBN 0-916700-51-8
    1. Afro-Americans—Religion.   2. Africa—Church history.
I. Altschul, Paisius, 1953-    .   II. Ancient Christianity and
African-America Conferences.
BR563.N4U53   1997
270'.089'96—dc21                                            97-38447
                                                               CIP

To
ABBOT HERMAN PODMOSHENSKY
and
HIEROMONK SERAPHIM ROSE

# CONTENTS

Contents

# ILLUSTRATIONS
(following page 52)

## HOLY IMAGES

Flight into Egypt
St. Cyprian of Carthage
St. Isaac
The Monastery of El Baramos
St. Moses the Black
SS. Apollo and Abib
St. John the Dwarf
St. Macarius the Great
SS. Irene and Sofia

## INHERITORS OF SUFFERING CHRISTIANITY

Nun Catherine working on the cover icon of St. Moses
Fr. Moses Berry
William Berry
Tombstone of William Berry
Caroline Boone Berry
Della Berry
Wallace White's cabin
Wallace and Daisy White, in front of their canebrake
Wallace White with members of the Missouri 6th Cavalry
Harrison White
Three of Wallace's daughters
Mamie's husband, Luther Berry
Charles Berry and his brother, Fred

ix

# INTRODUCTION: COMMON SUFFERING, COMMON WEALTH

*"Mother . . . little heart of mine, my joy, believe me, everyone is really responsible to all men for all men and for everything. I don't know how to explain it to you, but I feel it is so, painfully even. And how is it we went on then living, getting angry and not knowing?"*
—Elder Zosima, talking about his older brother, Markel before his death, in *The Brothers Karamazov* by Fyodor Dostoevsky

WE ALL SHARE in what has been passed down from Adam. Somehow, when we can face how our guilt, our ways, our past, our failings have contributed to the whole dilemma of human suffering, healing can begin. We are really all down here together. I look within, and I see that, unlike the self-deluded Pharisee in Jesus' parable, I *am* like other men. I look without, and I see that, unlike Cain, I *am* my brother's keeper. As Dostoevsky put it, I am responsible to you and for you. We share common sin, common pain, but also, common wealth.

We share in the effects of my parents' sins and your parents' sins, and my grandparents' sins and great-great-great. . . . It goes all the way back to Adam. Their sins visit us, entice us, allure us, and become a part of us. When I can own them as my own, deep release can come and we all can begin to change.

We also share in the inheritance of our parents—their virtues, their goodness, and their riches. Those things that enable us to go on. Those things that inspire. Those things that open up heaven. The true riches.

Yet the ground groans. We were made for Paradise, but we have settled for Nod, the land of wandering. The animals are afraid. They've felt something terrifying since the gaping rift of Man from his loving Maker. As Paradise gets further and further away, machines, drugs and pleasures try to soothe us into thinking that everything is really all right. We're progressing! Why it's virtually *like* reality! One of the ancient African Fathers, Anthony, spoke about our era. He said, "A time is coming when men will go mad, and when they see someone who is not mad, they will attack him saying, 'You are mad, you are not like us.'" We think that the people we see on the streets walking and talking to themselves don't quite fit. Those that are pounding their fists against the wall are just having a temporary spell of insanity. But perhaps it's deeper. Perhaps they are really saying, "I wasn't made for this as it is. I was made for something higher, something purer, something filled with Light."

Yet the children cry. "Little black boys and black girls" called "to join hands with little white boys and white girls and walk together as brothers and sisters" have tears instead. They endure constant fear, raging tides of questions, disappointments, and dampened love. Many are still hungry. Others are silent due to the terror of abuse. Many are tormented by the soul twists they endure in order to fit into the video violent vacuum that hammers at their peace a thousand times a day. "How long?" "Not long. . . ." "How long?" "Not long. . . ." Dr. Martin Luther King, Jr. consoles. How can he say that? Remember that Dr. King foresaw the Cross upon which he too would hang. He pointed to another path: the path of healing, the path of reconciliation, the path of life.

This common feeling, this common pathos that has affected us all, inspired AN UNBROKEN CIRCLE. This book emerged from four years of meeting together and sharing a common suffering that has gone deep enough, wide enough and rich enough to surround every one of us.

## The Conferences

Once during Matins, my godfather, Hieromonk Gerasim of the St. Herman of Alaska Brotherhood in Platina, California, prayerfully suggested the idea of having a conference on ancient Orthodox Christianity and its connection to and relevance for African-Americans. This past February we completed our fourth conference. The Ancient Christianity and African-America Conferences have all been held here at St. Mary of Egypt Orthodox Church and Reconciliation Ministries, at 31st and Troost in downtown Kansas City, Missouri, with the exception of the third, in 1996, which was hosted by The Joy of All Who Sorrow Eastern Orthodox Church in Indianapolis, Indiana. Since 1988 our building at 31st and Troost has served as a site for racial reconciliation and help for the homeless and strugglers on their spiritual journeys. In the past few years, over 40 of us have converted to the Eastern Orthodox Church.

The idea for the Conference was clear. The early Church in Africa was gathered around the Crucified Christ now risen from the dead. The path of the Cross *is* the path of life. The lectures showed that what the early Christians experienced in the catacombs and the coliseums of the Roman Empire, many African-American slaves experienced in the cotton fields and clandestine meetings of antebellum plantations. The suffering of the early Christian centuries produced the moral and mystical roots that enabled Christianity to flourish in the first millennium A.D. Likewise, the depth of faith and love, acquired by the slaves through their suffering, provides a link to a spiritual root system strong enough to transform willing souls in a corrupted American nation as we head into the third millennium A.D.

Drawing from the roots of Christianity in Africa, the lives of African saints of the early Church and those of African-American slaves that suffered for Christ, and from African-American spirituals and hymns, the lectures and talks of the four Conferences laid tracks on which future spiritual mothers and fathers might walk and hopefully form the reality of the spiritual world in the hearts of the next generation.

At a time when some feel that there are no spiritual solutions, lecture after lecture drew from the rivers of ancient Christianity and from the witness and wisdom of the slaves to give direction to the dilemmas of our present age. These spiritual rivers, which nourished the early Church, were flowing in and out of Africa. Having produced tens of thousands of martyrs in the first three centuries after Christ, the African Church led the way in preserving the vitality of the faith passed on from the martyrs when Christianity was legally tolerated after 313 A.D. At that time, African deserts became life-giving springs filled with tens of thousands of holy monks and virgins. As more and more Christians in the cities began to compromise politically, morally and economically, still others went to the deserts of Egypt and Ethiopia to repent and purify themselves. As they purified their hearts, they purified their families and nations as well. They did not retreat to lives of self-centered withdrawal. Rather, their guiding principle was that of Abraham in his intercession for Sodom: a few that repent can save a city.

## The Talks

AN UNBROKEN CIRCLE includes some of the lectures and testimonies presented at the Conferences.

*Fr. Antonious Conner* continues with further insight on this enormous subject with his overview of early African Christianity. Fr. Antonious, a Coptic Orthodox priest from St. Thomas, U.S. Virgin Islands, clearly shows how extensive the influence of African Christianity was on the rest of the developing Church.

*Fr. Jerome Sanderson,* an Orthodox priest and iconographer from Indianapolis, presents a panorama of the African presence in the early Church.

In my essay, I explore the vast influence that African monasticism has had on the rest of the world.

*Deacon Kinfu Dibawo,* from the Ethiopian Orthodox (Tewahedo) Church, provides an overview of the rich heritage of the Ethiopian Christians by tracing their movement of faith from King Solomon and the Queen of Sheba to His Imperial Majesty, Haile Selassie I, martyred in 1975.

*Nun Catherine,* Mother Superior of St. Xenia Metochion in Indianapolis and founder of the St. Andrew Rublev Iconography School, accents the quality of meekness necessary in our relationships with others and in our witness to the world system. In a very important distinction, she describes not only the meekness of humble, personal sacrifice, but also the meekness of a whole people, who with humble dependence upon God fought off an aggressor nation, as happened with Ethiopia's resistance of Italy in the battle of Aduwa.

*Fr. Moses Berry,* Orthodox priest and pastor of Christ the Good Shepherd Orthodox Church in St. Louis, Missouri, draws from his personal family history to show the deep, otherworldly Christianity that has been passed down from the righteous slaves who suffered in this country. But with his lecture comes a clear warning. Because of today's emphasis on making it in *this* world, many are in danger of losing the profound connection with the heavenly realm that so many of their forebears obtained at tremendous cost.

*Professor Albert Raboteau,* Professor of Religion at Princeton and author of *Slave Religion*[1] and *Fire in the Bones,*[2] gives an overview of the spiritual life the African slaves lived in America, its similarities with

ancient Orthodox Christianity and, finally, the importance that re-
claiming this heritage has for all Americans. He draws special attention to the "communion of saints." Those whom we can call on for
their prayers and assistance are not limited to our earthly contem-
poraries, but include as well that "great cloud of witnesses" in the
heavens, those that have gone before us.

*Monk Damascene Christensen,* priest-monk of the St. Herman of
Alaska Brotherhood and author of *Not of this World: the Life and
Teachings of Fr. Seraphim Rose,*[3] further delineates the links between
early Catacomb Christianity and the suffering faith of the slaves and
slave martyrs. Drawing from spirituals, slave narratives, and the
teaching of the ancient Church, he emerges with conclusions that
are both inspiring as well as challenging for those who want to draw
from the well of truth gained through suffering.

The four personal testimonies included demonstrate the applica-
tion of historical fact and spiritual teaching to the daily struggles of
life in the world.

*Carla N. Thomas, M.D.* provides an inspiring story of healing.
Starting with the unmercenary healing tradition of the Church, she
goes on to highlight Dr. Martin Luther King, Jr. as an unmercenary
*social* healer. She then pulls from her own life struggles what it
means today to be an unmercenary healer in a yet racially divided
society.

*Father Deacon Bishoy Cole* takes us on a journey from his gang-
banging days in LA to his discovery of the Orthodox Church and
African Christianity. With love for all that helped him on his way, he
now serves at Saints Abraham and Mary Coptic Orthodox Church in
St. Louis, Missouri.

*Marina Thompson,* one of the coordinators of the Conferences,
shares from her own spiritual path. She relates how she encountered God as a little girl, and how she was later healed of the devas-
tating effects of losing her mother when she was a teenager through
her discovery of the Orthodox Church.

*Michael Redmond,* a Reader at the St. Mary of Egypt Orthodox
Church, recounts the pain of growing up fatherless in a white-domi-
nated society, the numbness of his days on drugs, his joy of being a
father, and finally, his finding African fathers in the Church.

1. Albert J. Raboteau, *Slave Religion* (New York: Oxford University Press, Inc.,
1978).

2. Albert J. Raboteau, *A Fire in the Bones* (Boston: Beacon Press, 1995).

3. Fr. Damascene Christensen, *Not of This World* (Santa Rosa, Calif.: Seraphim Rose Foundation, 1993).

## Gleanings

After experiencing the Conferences—the talks, prayers, and sharing together—many impressions have emerged:

- The foundations of Christianity show that, from its origins, the Church has had a very strong African presence that exerted a primary influence on its development.
- Drawing from the well of African Christian history and African saints, we find an enormous depth of heritage in the Afro-American collective identity. This priceless heritage not only breaks down past prejudicial myths, but also points to forefathers and mothers, summits of sanctity who teach, inspire and challenge.
- The early African leader Tertullian said, "The blood of the martyrs is the seed of the Church." As the blood of the early martyrs sanctified the soil and the soul of their nations, so too, the suffering of the American slave martyrs and confessors has sanctified this soil, and even now is crying out for the transformation of the soul of this nation. They form a part of that "great cloud of witnesses," and they provide one of the strongest spiritual resources available to us for inspiration today.
- As our national soul becomes increasingly captive to the consumerist pleasure-seeking that lies at the foundation of our popular culture, the need for a transformative ascetic path becomes ever more acute. Prayer, fasting, deeds of repentance and mercy, as modeled by the African desert fathers and mothers, enable each individual's personal roots to deepen so as to provide the internal strength to endure. That which St. Moses of Ethiopia, St. Mary of Egypt and St. Anthony of Egypt gained in the desert is waiting for this generation of fathers and mothers to apprehend.
- Rather than trying to hide like ostriches from prevailing racial injustice, we can, through the path of prayer:
  *face* it in ourselves and our past;
  *seek* to gain forgiveness, as we change, from those we offend and have offended;
  *forgive* the people that have wounded us; and then,
  *release* righteous anger at the demons that continue to perpetrate injustice and self-destruction in these times, purposing to work together to release ourselves and others, through our Lord Jesus Christ. As St. Macarius the Great said,
  *"If we shall remember the evil that men have done us, the remembrance of God will grow weak in us; but if we shall remember the evil brought upon us by the demons, we shall be safe from their arrows."*

Long ago, St. Paul the Apostle taught us, "Be angry and sin not." (Eph. 4:26) And "we wrestle not against flesh and blood, but against . . . spiritual wickedness in high places." (Eph. 6:12) Anger that has been turned on ourselves and others now can, and should, be redirected towards the spiritual and ideological forces behind the injustices.

May the lessons that we are learning mature in us. May we gain more answers for ourselves and those around us as we continue to look back into the treasures of the Church. May each of us find the peace that comes through the Cross of our Lord Jesus Christ for our families, our communities, and ourselves.

*Fr. Paisius Altschul*
St. Mary of Egypt Orthodox Church
February 20, 1997

# AN UNBROKEN CIRCLE

# 1
# AFRICAN ROOTS

# 1

# OVERVIEW OF ANCIENT CHRISTIANITY IN AFRICA

## FR. ANTONIOUS CONNER

THE BIBLE RECORDS THE STORY of God's unfolding drama of Redemption. We all know that the supreme act of Redemption is Christ crucified on the Cross for all humanity, no matter where one is from. All people from every race, every ethnic group of Humanity need to be redeemed. Every group needs to hear and understand God's word of Redemption as is seen in our Lord Jesus Christ.

From its beginning to its end, the Bible provides information about God's dealing with numerous nations, peoples, and tongues. Of the many people who are mentioned and highlighted in the Scriptures, many are black people, African people. And we, too, are objects of God's redeeming grace. We, too, were and are vessels whom God uses to spread His redemptive message to the world. Therefore, it is important for African-Americans to appreciate the presence of people of color in the Scriptures and their contribution to Christianity.

Why is this important? The Bible is recorded history from God's perspective. It is reliable, and it is a framework in which the human race can gain eternal salvation. If we as a people were ignorant of our history and its heritage, we would walk blindly into the future as African-Americans. Far too many of our people reject Christianity and the Bible because they do not understand that it speaks about *us* and about our experience. I believe that it is time for us, as African people, to read, to study, and to draw lessons for ourselves from those things which God has ordained to be written about African people in His Word. I would like to caution you, though, that the African presence in the Bible and in history and its contribution is in no way the entire focus of the Bible or Christian history. Its contributions, however, should not be neglected or despised. Like other peoples, Africans, too, should learn to appreciate God's word, which is addressed *to* them and *about* them as a people.

## Prophecy

The Orthodox Church in Africa, especially the Coptic [i.e., Egyptian] Orthodox Church, is unique in its establishment. This very establishing was a subject of prophecy in 750 B.C. by Isaiah the Prophet. This can be found in Isaiah 19:19: "In that day there will be an altar to the Lord in the midst of the land of Egypt and a pillow at its border."

A subject of prophecy—the establishment of the Church in Africa! We know that when Isaiah said that there shall be "an altar to the Lord in the midst of the land of Egypt and a pillow at its border" he could not be talking about a Jewish altar, because at that time you could only have an altar inside of Jerusalem, the place of worship and temple for the Hebrew race. We also know that it was not a pagan altar, for Isaiah is plain and clear, saying, "an altar to the Lord." Thus, we see a very clear prophecy concerning the establishment of Christianity in Africa. Isaiah gives us more details in Isaiah 19:1:

> Behold, the Lord rideth upon a swift cloud, and shall come into Egypt, and the idols of Egypt shall be moved at His Presence.

These prophecies and promises were fulfilled by the flight of the holy family into Egypt from the tyrant, King Herod the Great. The holy family found refuge among these Africans. Thus our Lord Jesus Christ came to Egypt during His childhood, to establish himself as the foundation stone for His Church.

The Church in Alexandria, Egypt became one of the four primary Christian sees in the world, among the churches of Jerusalem, Antioch, and Rome, joined only later by Constantinople. Saint Cyril the Great of Alexandria interpreted this prophecy, saying,

> The glittering cloud that carried the child Jesus to Egypt was his mother, Saint Mary, who surpassed the cloud in purity. The altar that

was established in the midst of the land of Egypt is the Christian Church, that has replaced the temples of paganism, as the idols collapsed and the temples were dispersed in the presence of the Lord.

Egypt, as we know quite well, was the mother of civilization and learning in ancient times and has now become the mother of spirituality and blessing to the rest of the world, and deserving of the Lord's Word spoken by Isaiah the prophet, "Blessed be my people Egypt." (Is. 19:25) Other prophecies were to be fulfilled concerning our Lord Jesus Christ and this people, the African people, in whom He found welcome hearts. Hosea prophesied, saying, "I called My Son out of Egypt." David, in Psalm 68:31, stated, "Ethiopia will stretch out her hands to God." Did you know that before the Lord went to Egypt there were prophecies that African kings were to be among the first among the nations of the world to know about His birth, and to come to worship Him, and to offer Him gifts? King David prophesied in Psalm 72:10: "The kings of Sheba and Seba [i.e., ancient Ethiopia] will offer gifts." Isaiah also prophesied concerning this in Is. 60:5-6:

> The wealth of the nations shall come to you, a multitude of camels shall cover you. The young camels of Midian and Ephah, all those of Sheba shall come, they shall bring gold and frankincense, and shall proclaim the praise of the Lord.

Was this fulfilled? Yes, among the wise men, there was an African named Balthasar. These Magi believed and thus they saw the star. They came from long distances to worship the Lord Jesus Christ. These are the beginning roots of African Christianity in the prophecies of the Bible, and their subsequent fulfillment.

I have had the blessing of visiting Ethiopia and living in Egypt, as well as visiting some of these sites where the holy family stayed. When the holy family went all the way down into Egypt, the Christ Child was about two years old. Many families embraced them and took care of them because they did not travel on the main road. Herod and his soldiers had pursued them quite some way into Egypt. But, as you can imagine, with idols falling down in pagan Egypt, if a family was to come and the idols were to start falling, this miraculous news would quickly spread. They would tell people, "There is a child, there is a woman and a donkey, and a child and a man leading them, and miraculous things are happening, idols are falling down, and Herod is pursuing them." Thus, their journey through Egypt was very precarious. They went as far down as El Maharaq, which today is literally in the midst of Egypt. There the Child was placed on a rock, a small stone, inside of a home. In the third

5

century, they built up some stucco on the rock, to be able to place a slab for an altar on top. I have had the blessing of going to this place and praying there myself. It is called Saint Mary's Monastery. If you have a chance to visit Africa, go and visit some of these holy sites.

## The New Testament

Did you know that when the Lord started His ministry one of the twelve Apostles was an African? Symeon, who was honorably called the Canaanite because of his ancestors, was from Ham through Canaan. The African Canaanites dominated Palestine, originally called the Land of Canaan, years before Abraham or any of his descendants existed. The Apostle Simon, prior to meeting Christ, belonged to a faction of zealots whose objectives were to expel Romans from Palestine by advocating armed revolution. However, after becoming a follower of the Messiah, the converted African Canaanite changed his stand and became an Apostle of God's love. Symeon (or Simon) was a Jew by nationality and by culture, but not through genealogy, since he was a descendent from Ham. One of Christ's first twelve Apostles—an African, did you know that?

Let us also remember, and not forget, Simon of Cyrene [in modern Libya]. This African was compelled to share Christ's burden of the Cross toward the Place of the Skull, to Calvary. It's quite amazing about an African helping Christ carry the Cross. He did not just happen to be there on the day of Crucifixion, for he was a follower and a disciple. He was part of a vibrant movement of Africans who believed in Christ and were living in Jerusalem at that time. His devotion was such that he followed Christ with his two sons, Alexander and Rufus, as Saint Mark identifies in his Gospel. (Mk. 15:21) Alexander and Rufus were strong and effective preachers of the Gospel and became leaders in the Church. Saint Paul the Apostle saluted Rufus because of his devotion to the ministry. He said, "Greet Rufus chosen in the Lord, and his mother, and mine." (Rom. 16:13) Saint Paul would not have said this if he did not know about the virtue and the devotion, not only of Rufus, but also of his mother.

There were in early Christianity many other Africans who became disciples, prophets, and teachers. Another Symeon, who was called Niger, after his homeland, and Lucius of Cyrene, were both prophets in the Antiochian Church, located in Syria. Did you know that it was by these men from Africa that God chose to have hands laid on the great Saints Paul and Barnabas for their apostolic work? For in Acts 13:1-2 it is stated, "And there were dwelling in Antioch prophets and teachers," and it lists Lucius of Cyrene and Symeon the

Niger. It goes on to say, "Separate for me Barnabas and Paul to the work to which I have called them." God used Africans to commission this great apostolic missionary work.

There are, of course, many other African Christians mentioned in the New Testament, such as the woman of great faith, the Canaanite, in Matthew 15:22. At Pentecost, the birthday of the Church, every nation under heaven was there, including those from Africa. Acts 2:10 reveals that men from Egypt and parts of Libya adjoining Cyrene were present, and it is well known historically that Ethiopians were also there. We cannot forget, as well, that it was by divine providence that Philip was sent to the African Ethiopian eunuch as recounted in Acts, chapter 8. This eunuch was a man of great authority, a finance minister under Queen Candace of Ethiopia, a large and a great nation at that time. Indeed, whatever they might be called—Africans, Hammites, Canaanites, Cushites, or even Semites—we have to remember that black Africans were part of the population in Palestine and were a part of Christianity from its very beginning.

## John Mark

Continuing our overview of early Christianity, let's now consider the prominent place that John Mark held in the formation of the African Church. John Mark was a native of North Africa, from a northern country, which we now call Libya. He was born of Jewish parentage in the city of Cyrene in Pentapolis, west of the northern border of Egypt. He was known to many as simply "Mark." As such, he has been honored as one of the Gospel evangelists, numbered with Matthew, Luke, and John.

According to history, John Mark and his mother moved from Africa to Palestine after having been robbed. There are references to them in Palestine in the New Testament. "And they gathered in the house of Mary, the mother of John Mark." (Acts 12:12) This home is the traditional site of the institution of the Lord's supper. It is also believed that this is the same house where Pentecost took place. The young man referred to by Christ when He sent His disciples to go and find a place for the Passover, who would be carrying a jug, a water pot, on his head, is believed to be John Mark.

John Mark himself labored tremendously with Saint Paul and Barnabas in Antioch, Cyprus, Asia Minor, and Rome. Even the people of Venice consider him to be their patron saint. After the contention concerning John Mark between the Holy Apostles Barnabas and Paul, Barnabas (his uncle) took John Mark and sailed to Cyprus. We know from history that Barnabas received his martyrdom, and John Mark was there to pick up the body and to help to put it in a cave and bury it. He then sailed to Alexandria, Egypt.

Alexandria, that great ancient metropolis, was named after Alexander the Great, the Macedonian conqueror. It was home to many different types of philosophies and schools. Its library was the largest in the ancient world. As John Mark was walking through the city, one of his sandals became loose and broke. He went to a cobbler by the name of Anianus to mend it. As the cobbler was mending the sandal, the awl went into his hand, and then he bawled out, "The One God!" John Mark, in surprise at this cobbler's cry "The One God," searched and found some clay. As he put it on the man's hand, he said, "About this One God, do you know his Son, the Lord Jesus Christ?" and miraculously healed the cobbler's wound. John Mark then went to Anianus' house and converted him and his family, and they were baptized. This happened around about 42 A.D. Some people put it as late as 61 A.D., closer to the martyrdoms of SS. Peter and Paul in Rome, because John Mark had gone back up to Rome and labored with Peter, his cousin. Another time, Paul requests his assistance when he asks that Timothy "Take Mark and bring him with thee: for he is profitable to me for the ministry." (2 Ti. 4:11)

Anianus the cobbler became a priest, and later a bishop, with other priests and deacons who were ordained by John Mark in Egypt. Because of the increasing Roman and pagan persecution against the growing Church in Egypt, the Apostle had to leave able leadership behind. At the urging of the faithful, he went back to Rome around 65 A.D. John Mark was in Rome at the time of the martyrdoms of Peter and Paul. In 68 A.D., John Mark went back down to this budding and growing church in Alexandria.

During this period, on the day of the feast of the Resurrection, he was about to enter into a home that had been made into a church for services. All of a sudden, pagan Romans saw him and took him away by force. This particular year the feast of the Resurrection had fallen at the time of a pagan festival and they wanted to offer sacrifices to their gods. They grabbed John Mark, tied a rope around his stomach, dragged him through the city of Alexandria for a day, and then put him into prison.

After this first torture and imprisonment, God miraculously healed him. An angel appeared to him and told him that now he was going to have peace. As he was about to communicate with the angel, he saw Christ also, Who told him "Now you are going to your peace."

When the soldiers came back, they saw that he was well. They then put a rope around his neck and dragged him through the city until he was decapitated. This is how John Mark received the crown of blessed martyrdom in Alexandria, Egypt in 68 A.D.

His primary labor lay in preaching and performing many miracles as he traveled throughout Africa: through Egypt, through the oasis and the desert of Libya, through Upper Egypt in the south, where the Nile River flows down from the southern mountains.

Until this day, his remains are in Egypt, in the main cathedral of Saint Mark in Alexandria and in the new cathedral in Cairo. Because the Venetians consider St. Mark as their patron saint, some visiting merchants from Venice stole part of the headless body in the eighth century. It wasn't until recently, during the papacy of His Holiness of blessed memory, Pope Kyrillos VI of the Coptic Orthodox Church, that through negotiation with the Vatican in Rome, the relics were returned. The head has always remained in Egypt.

## The African Christian Empire

This, then, is the beginning of the ecclesiastical aspect of the Church in Africa, with the apostle John Mark ordaining Anianus as bishop of Egypt before his own martyrdom in 68 A.D.

From Church history, we know that St. Matthew went to Ethiopia, and that when he arrived on the eastern shore he found many Ethiopian Christians. Their faith in Christ was traced to some Ethiopians being present in Jerusalem for the first Pentecost. As a result, St. Matthew did not ordain anyone or establish the Church. It wasn't until the early fourth century, in 329 A.D., that Athanasius, our twentieth patriarch, ordained Frumentius as bishop to go and administer over the Ethiopians.

In this period, Christianity spread quickly as far as Nubia and Sudan. The African Christian Empire that developed around the fourth century was comprised of Egypt, Nubia, Sudan, and Ethiopia. From what we understand about religious belief at that time in Egypt, one can see how it would be within the Egyptian worldview to accept Jesus Christ, even as a child. Other teachings about Christ and His Church, such as the immortality of the soul, the resurrection of the body, the judgment of the soul, one supreme God, and the Trinity, had some references within Egyptian religion. We have seen even in recent times confirmation of these truths due to the archaeological excavations of some Egyptian tombs. There are found many types of symbols of life, and the belief in the immortality of the soul and its resurrection. The Egyptians embalmed their dead because they believed in the resurrection of the body and after-life of the soul.

## Martyrdom

After the martyrdom of St. Mark, the Church in Africa, especially in Egypt, enjoyed a relative period of peace until 203 A.D., when Emperor Septimius Severus issued an edict forbidding conversion to both Christianity and Judaism. Christianity at that time had grown very rapidly and Rome felt that it had to be eliminated. A series of persecutions were instituted in order to suppress the growth of Christianity, which openly defied the worship of the emperors. In their persecution of Christians, the Romans frequently concentrated on Egypt for several reasons. First, the Church in Alexandria and its schools were attracting the philosophers to this new faith. Second, Alexandria represented a vital center for providing the Roman capital with products, and for this reason the emperors were afraid of any revolution in Egypt. Finally, the courage of the Egyptian Christians and their stern desire to attain the crown of martyrdom so perplexed the persecutors that the Emperor Diocletian himself came to Alexandria to practice persecution. He had heard about these Christians in Egypt and in the rest of Africa—that when persecuted, they would not fight back. He wondered, "How can these people stand up like this for this Christian faith?" So he decided to go to Egypt to personally supervise and participate in the tortures as Emperor. Those that were persecuted were subjected to very innovative and various tortures, regardless of their age or sex.

The most severe and bloody period of the Coptic Church, or the period of the most persecution, was when this same Diocletian issued an order that all the churches were to be demolished; all scriptures were to be burned; and all Christians who were not officially so before, were to be made slaves. This intense period of persecution resulted in the widespread torture and martyrdom of millions of Christians, because of their courageous testimony for Christ. The Coptic Christians consider the beginning of Diocletian's military ascent to the throne as the beginning of the era of the Coptic martyrs. This marks the start of the Coptic calendar known in the western world as *Anno Martyr*. Whenever you hear the word A.M., or Era of Martyrs, it is because the African Egyptian Christians decided to start their Holy Year by commemorating the Era of Martyrs.

The Egyptian Church maintains selected bibliographies of martyrs and saints that are full of stories of these courageous ones, whose blood became the seed of the church. These books represent only a fraction of their lives, a few of which follow. Saint Sophia, a native of ancient Memphis in middle Egypt, was martyred at that time. Her body was later removed to Constantinople by Emperor Constantine. Saint Damiana, a daughter of a governor of the northern province of the Delta, established a monastery with forty virgins and all were massacred by Diocletian. The site of her nunnery and martyrdom is still inhabited by nuns and is a favorite pilgrimage center up until this day. Saint Catherine of Alexandria was martyred at the early age of eighteen by Maximus in 307 A.D. The famous monastery at Mount Sinai still bears her name. There is St. Mina, a martyr of the third century, whose famous monastery near Alexandria is still in existence.

There are millions of African martyred saints: Egyptians, Nubians, Sudanese, and Ethiopians, who lost their lives during the great era of persecution. The African Church had clear vision that was open to eternity. She had a lofty concept of martyrdom. To die as a martyr was not considered as death or as something terrible, but rather as a new birth, an entry into paradise. This is why so many Africans were able to endure martyrdom. For them it was a deep blessing.

## Further Contributions

In 313 A.D. Constantine the Great issued the Great Edict of Tolerance. The African Church entered a new era under Byzantine rule that was to last until the Islamic conquest in 641. Christianity was officially recognized in Egypt, Nubia, Sudan, and Ethiopia. With this new freedom, the Church experienced rapid growth as a result of the mass conversion of pagans to the Christian faith.

With the end of the legal persecutions came the rise of monasticism. Monasticism is one of Egypt's greatest gifts to the world, one of the sweet fruits of the African. Africa obtained this fruit from the persecution against the Coptic Christians. It is well known that the star of the desert is Saint Anthony the Great of Upper Egypt, who established the monastic movement and is considered the "Father of Monasticism."

Another great African contribution to the Church was the catechetical school of Alexandria. During the early centuries of the Christian Church worldwide, the first and most famous catechetical school was that of Alexandria, called the *Didascalium*. It was an important light and a means of instruction for the Christian faith. It offered instructions in Christian faith and theology, along with the study of civil sciences such as philosophy, medicine, physics, chem-

11

istry, astronomy, physiology, mathematics, geometry, history, music, and ancient and modern language. It was open to catechumens—those who believed in Christ but had not yet been baptized and needed instruction on how to live as Christians—as well as to deacons and Christian students who desired a deeper knowledge and understanding of the Christian doctrine and faith. It was also open to pagan students who were still searching for the truth. According to tradition, Saint Mark is the one who opened up this first catechetical school. Saint Mark, having grown up in Africa before moving back to Palestine and Jerusalem, was himself multilingual and very well learned in Greek and Latin. Before his martyrdom he realized that the only way to be able to counteract the overwhelming philosophical and pagan influences prevalent in Alexandria and the known world at the time was to be able to open up a school. It happened to be located where the main cathedral is today in Alexandria. The school developed and expanded under the great African deans, philosophers, and teachers of theology, such as Athenagoras, St. Clement of Alexandria, St. Athanasius, and St. Didymus the Blind, to name a few. Origen, with his multitudinous volumes on Holy Scriptures, is well known. Although he later fell into error, he undoubtedly made a substantive contribution to Christian education and study of the Scriptures. Graduates from other theological schools in other parts of the Christian world later came to study in the school of Alexandria, including Saint Gregory the Theologian, Saint Basil the Great, St. John Chrysostom, Saint Jerome, and Rufinus. Thus, the school in Alexandria became a lighthouse for Christianity for a span of five centuries until the reign of Justinian, in 529 A.D. After 451 and the council of Chalcedon, the main learning center for the Coptic church was transferred to the monastery of Saint Macarius in the Wadi Natrun Desert, where it continued for several centuries.

## The Councils

While the rest of Egypt was being Christianized and the monastic movement was spreading, heresies within the Church began to arise and threatened to undermine the very essence of Orthodox Christianity worldwide. Battles for the holy Orthodox and apostolic church and faith were being raged in Alexandria, and in ecclesiastical centers throughout the Christian world. The end of persecution had brought not only growth and expansion to the Church, but also an ideal climate for dissension and heresy. As a result of the heresies, the Christian Church saw a need to define her doctrine more clearly, and to formulate her creed and faith. The Egyptian Church was an important part of the first three Ecumenical Councils, fighting to put a stop to the heresies and formulating Orthodox creeds, doctrines, and documents of the apostolic canons of the Church.

The first Ecumenical Council was convened at Nicea in 325 A.D. The issue at hand was the false teaching of Arius, who regarded Christ as a created being rather than God. Because Arius, a Libyan priest, was popular and clever, many had been led astray. Three hundred and eighteen bishops, including the nineteenth Coptic patriarch, Pope Alexander, with twenty of his bishops and his gifted deacon, Athanasius, attended the council. Saint Athanasius, who had a long time struggle with Arius and his followers, skillfully defended the Orthodox faith. The Council refuted the Arian heresy, affirmed the divinity of Christ, and formulated the Nicene Creed.

People occasionally ask the question, "What contribution did Africa make to Christianity?" Wherever you go, whether you're a Methodist or a Lutheran, you read the Nicene Creed, and say, "We believe in one God, the Father Almighty . . ." It's in everybody's prayer books worldwide: Greek, Russian, everybody knows about the Creed, the Nicene Creed. It was penned primarily by St. Athanasius, an African from Egypt. This Creed, which was adhered to by the Coptic Church and the rest of the world, and which was composed by an African, is used by the entire Church, both East and West, until this day. It was not only worded by Athanasius himself, but also by Patriarch Alexander, and Longinus, the bishop of Caesaria in Cappadocia. It was approved and signed by the members of the Council.

The Second Ecumenical Council was held at Constantinople in 381 A.D. and attended by one hundred fifty bishops. It included an Alexandrian delegation led by Abba Timotheus, the twenty-second Patriarch. The Council was convened to refute another heresy being proclaimed by Macedonius, a bishop of Constantinople who denied the divinity of the Holy Spirit. It affirmed the divinity of the Holy Spirit, and added the last clauses of the Nicene Creed, concerning the Holy Spirit; the One, Holy, Universal and Apostolic Church; the one baptism; the awaiting of the resurrection of the dead; and eternal life.

At the Third Ecumenical Council at Ephesus, in 431 A.D., the holy bishops considered the heresy of Nestorius, a bishop of Constantinople. This council was attended by two hundred bishops. Among them was Pope Kyrillos the First, the twenty-fourth Patriarch of the Church of Alexandria, known as the "Pillar of Faith." He had previously convened, in Alexandria itself, two local councils for the bishops. He was the head of his own See in Alexandria and circulated many letters concerning the Nestorian heresy. It was Saint Kyrillos who worded the introduction to the Creed, which was first affirmed and accepted by the Council of Alexandria and which is still recited by the Copts as a prefix to the Athanasian [Nicene] Creed until this day. The Council, under the presidency of Saint Cyril [Kyrillos], condemned the teaching of Nestorius and excommunicated him. It reaffirmed the perfect union of Christ's divinity with his humanity, and acknowledged the Virgin Mary as the Theotokos, the Birthgiver, the Bearer of God. We see here Africans in leadership in the early ecumenical world.

## Witness and Mission

The African Church did a tremendous amount of work in preaching and missionary activity. The mere fact that Saint Mark preached in Egypt to the Egyptian Christians has resulted in the Copts being very emphatic about missionary activity in the character of the Church. The African Church had individuals as well as groups serving as witnesses and missionaries.

A spectacular example of witnessing to the Christian faith was the Theban Legions. These 6,000 soldiers were from Thebes, presently in Luxor in Upper Egypt. They were sent by Diocletian to Gaul [France] and Switzerland, to quell rebellion. The force was led by St. Maurice, who earned martyrdom together with all of the soldiers of the legion, for refusing to sacrifice to an idol. In Switzerland, you can still see today a statue of Saint Maurice in one of the public squares. It is well known that the Theban Legions were the first to bring the Christian faith to certain areas of Switzerland and France. St. Maurice and his legions were followed by missionaries who were led as far as Lake Zurich, where they baptized and converted many people until they themselves became martyrs.

In the legion was one called Verena, from Upper Egypt. Spared from the martyrdom, she spent the rest of her life in present-day Switzerland, educating people to become Christian, and teaching them about the principles of hygiene. She is portrayed in some icons as having in one hand a water jug and in the other a comb. Even today Swiss housewives venerate St. Verena as their matron saint.

The Coptic African missionaries reached as far as the British Isles long before the arrival of Saint Augustine of Canterbury in 597 A.D. In African Christian history, we find that seven Egyptian monks went to Ireland for the preaching of the Gospel of Christ and were martyred there. These seven monks are still recognized in Irish history.

14

Ecclesiastical history is impregnated with captivating accounts of Egyptian and other African Christians who preached Christianity in the north and to the west, to South Africa, Arabia, Persia, India, Europe.

## An Invitation

Now, such truths and facts concerning the authenticity, the apostolicity, and the contribution of the ancient African Church are liberating to many of us. They should serve to demonstrate to us, and to those who say that Christianity is a white man's religion, that it is not true. Christianity is not necessarily black, and it is not necessarily white, nor is it yellow, but I am saying that these facts should serve to help African-Americans develop a sense of identity—as African-American Christians. For the most part, because of what has occurred in American history, African-Americans have felt, "What contribution has Africa made to Christianity?" They don't know about this great history and the contribution of the African Church. Discovering this and realizing all these different contributions—the great catechetical schools, the martyrs, missionaries, the date for the celebration of Pascha (Easter), the first use of the title of "Pope"— all these different things, in Africa? This can give not only a sense of identity, but also more importantly, a real and true sense of a crucial and a cordial invitation to Christ and His Church. The truth remains that each person, regardless of racial and ethnic origin, or whatever contribution his or her nation might have made, must personally come to the Lord for salvation. Faith in the atoning death of Christ is the way to redemption from sin and to a holistic liberation, for any nation. And it was and should be a holistic liberation for the African-American people. Of course, it is not a claim to be from any nation that is going to save an individual. I say, nonetheless, that we cannot deny the contribution of the African Church, in terms of what she has done, and her people, and what she continues today to do in terms of Christianity. Finally, we always have to say, "To God be the glory!"

# 2

# AFRICAN PILLARS OF THE CHURCH

FR. JEROME SANDERSON

WHEN I WAS A YOUNG MAN, a Moslem told me that Christianity was a white man's religion. He said that Islam was the true religion for blacks because it came from Africa. Over the years I have heard other variations on this theme. I heard, for instance, that blacks were adopted into Christianity. I heard that Christianity was foisted upon blacks during slavery. If I added to that the European images of Christ and Christianity in literature, art and movies, it became quite apparent that Jesus, the saints and even the angels seemed to be Caucasians. As a teenager, I saw the movie *King of Kings*. Not only was Jesus blond with piercing blue eyes but there was no one in the whole movie with so much as a good tan!

This subject may seem petty and distasteful to some. Nevertheless, the lie continues. Today many black youths are still told that Christianity is not natural to them. They are told that they don't belong— that it's the slavemaster's religion. Color is a barrier to them.

In the West, Christians of African descent have been deprived of the rich treasury of saintly lives that could inspire them. They need holy images, heroes and models that they can identify with. In many cases, to know that some of the saints were black or African and were revered for centuries by the Christian world may be just the key to open the gateway to true piety and love of God. The central role played by Africa and Africans in the formation of the Church

16

has not been taught to most African-American Christians. By introducing them to Africa's influence in the early Church, we introduce them to the rich history of saints, holy and righteous ones who adorned it. By acquainting them with the truth of Christian history, we arm them against the onslaught of deceit, misinformation and ignorance. We link them to the early Church through their forefathers.

The following are only a few of the lives of saints, people of color, who have graced the Church. All of them are formative figures in her development.

## Saints Perpetua and Felicity

In the second century, the Church was being persecuted in Rome and Greece. The emperors pursued the Christians all over the world, wherever they were. In about 193 A.D., in Carthage (a city in North Africa, now a suburb of Tunis), there were at one time twelve martyrs. Of them, Perpetua and Felicity are particularly revered today. Perpetua was of a noble family and had just had a child. Felicity, who had given birth while in prison awaiting martyrdom, and her husband, Satyrus, were with her in jail. Perpetua had a number of vivid dreams and visions. In one she saw a ladder rising up to heaven, its rungs covered with knives, hooks, nails and other sharp instruments. At its foot was a great serpent. She saw Satyrus run up the ladder without harm, and when he reached the top, he turned and called, "Perpetua, I'm waiting for you! Come on up but watch out for the serpent!" Perpetua mounted the ladder and stepped on the serpent's head. At the end of her climb, she beheld a most beautiful world. Greatly awed, she told the others to come and they followed.

This dream was fulfilled the next day. The guards released wild beasts. Satyrus was bitten in the neck by a leopard and thus gained his martyr's crown. A bull gored Perpetua and Felicity, but Perpetua had been praying so fervently that she, immersed in heavenly thoughts, was unaware of the attack. When they were returned to the jail, she asked, "When are they going to release the animals on us?" Her comrades informed her that it had already happened and showed her where she had been gored. Later they went out again and the people called for them to be beheaded. The gladiator who came to her was so nervous and confused that he could not carry out the sentence, so Perpetua guided his sword and put it to her own heart to encourage him. Thus she was martyred. The rest followed soon after.

## Saint Cyprian of Carthage

At about this time there was a great leader in Carthage, named
Cyprian. He had studied rhetoric and philosophy in school and become a well-known teacher of these subjects. In his forty-sixth year,
after his conversion by a priest named Caelilius, he became a Christian. His zeal was so great that within a few years he was made
bishop of Carthage. During his bishopric, St. Cyprian guided the
African church through the ravages of a deadly plague that took a
great toll on the Roman Empire. He also strengthened and supported his flock during the Valerian persecutions. He was a prolific
writer, with a very melodic and sweet style. In 258 A.D., the persecution of the Church gained great momentum. Cyprian formed
what was called the "Underground Church"—the Catacomb
Church in Carthage. The Roman authorities ceaselessly persecuted
and hunted him. Constantly in flight, he ministered to his flock
wherever he could. At one point, when asked why he didn't simply
give himself up, he replied, "The white rose of labor can be as sweet
as the red rose of martyrdom." When he was finally caught and condemned to execution by beheading, St. Cyprian's only words were
"Thank you, Father." He was possessed of such a noble spirit that he
gave the executioner twenty-five pieces of gold and then joyfully
placed his head on the block for beheading.

## Saint Athanasius the Great

This great pillar and doctor of the church was born in Alexandria
in 296 A.D. As a youth he was spotted by Bishop Alexander of Alexandria, who had a home overlooking the ocean. One day the bishop
noticed that the young Athanasius and a group of other boys appeared to be playing church on the beach. One lad was baptizing
another. Concerned that they were making a game of something
very sacred and holy, Bishop Alexander summoned the boys and
gently reprimanded them for their careless presumption. Athanasius responded to this accusation in a surprising way. The boys, he
said, were not playing but were quite in earnest: the one being baptized was truly accepting Christ and seeking rebirth into His Body.
After hearing this eloquent response, the bishop chrismated the
newly baptized boy, and recognizing a divine calling in Athanasius,
arranged with his parents for him to be raised from then on in the
bishop's residence.

Athanasius accompanied Bishop Alexander to the First Ecumenical Council in Nicea, in 325. Even though he was only a deacon at

the time, he won the high regard of all with his brilliant contributions to the debates, which flabbergasted the heretical followers of Arius and strengthened the Orthodox.

With the passing of Bishop Alexander, Athanasius became the Archbishop of Alexandria, a position he held for over forty years. These were very tumultuous years, during which he endured condemnation, persecution, battles within the Church, flight from his enemies, and banishment. Throughout, whatever his trials, he continued to guide his flock. Athanasius also wrote many books and letters, including the *Life of St. Anthony*, a classic of spiritual literature. Athanasius often visited Anthony and was greatly strengthened and inspired by the holy life of this great light of the desert. Thousands were drawn to monastic endeavor through this book, and it has remained a major influence on the development of monasticism worldwide.

Banished five times from his see, St. Athanasius was able to minister to his flock in peace for only the last few years before his death in 373.

## Saint Anthony the Great

This radiant star of the desert was born in the village of Qwemen-el-Arons in the interior of Egypt, in about 250 A.D. His parents died when he was a young man, leaving Anthony and his sister great wealth. One day at church, Anthony heard the gospel verse "If you would be perfect go sell what you have and give to the poor—then you will have treasure in heaven," and it made an enormous impression on him. After providing for his sister, he gave away the remainder of his fortune, and went to stay for a while with some righteous Christians who lived very simply on the outskirts of town.

As time went on he was compelled by the Spirit towards a deeper asceticism and so moved into an old mausoleum in a cemetery. There he waged spiritual battle against Satan and against his own passions. Satan tried many strategies in his assault against Anthony, but the latter, through the grace of God, was victorious. Moved by the Spirit again, Anthony went deeper into the desert and found an abandoned fortress. There he remained for twenty years, praying unceasingly, struggling against demons and his own desires and striving to love God with all his heart, soul, mind, and strength. After a while, it began to be known that something wonderful was happening in that desert outpost. People began to gather at Anthony's enclosure, seeking wisdom, direction and healing. At times he would speak to them from within the fortress and, despite the fact that he would allow no one to see his face, his fame spread. The crowds around him grew. Eventually their eagerness to see Anthony compelled them to break down the door separating them from him and Anthony emerged from his place of struggle. It was supposed that he would appear weak and wasted after so many years of fasting and extreme self-denial. Instead, Anthony emerged looking radiant and healthy, lean but strong. With great love and compassion the saint taught, comforted and healed, nourishing his followers with spiritual direction. He was famous throughout the known world, and became advisor to bishops, and even to the Emperor Constantine. Those who sought to emulate his way of life built cells in the desert so that they might receive daily from this rich fount of heavenly grace, whose students included SS. Hilarion the Great and Macarius the Great, as well as Athanasius.

During a period of persecution, Anthony was moved to leave his desert hermitage and go to Alexandria, there to strengthen the struggling Church. He hoped that he, too, would receive the crown of martyrdom. While in the city, he healed the sick, made many converts and went freely among the prisoners and those slated for martyrdom, encouraging and strengthening them. The authorities feared Anthony and wanted nothing to do with him and thus the crown of martyrdom eluded him.

The gifts of the Spirit were well manifest in this righteous one, who came as close to perfection as is humanly possible. Illiterate and unlettered, he was made wise by God, and so confounded the worldly and educated. St. Anthony saw distant happenings clairvoyantly and could perceive the inner character of each man's soul. Always acting with profound love and fatherly tenderness, he cast out demons and performed healings. His life became a model for God-seekers in all ages and places. St. Anthony spent eighty-five years in the desert and entered into his rest in the year 356.

## Saint Mary of Egypt

The life of St. Mary of Egypt is told by Father Zosima, an African monk and ascetic. Because of his advancements in spiritual struggle, he began to think of himself as having attained the heights in Christian virtue. Zosima was inspired to go to a monastery in Palestine, and during his first Lent there he journeyed 20 days into the desert to fast and pray. One day he saw out of the corner of his eye a human figure, dark and naked. He gave chase, but it fled from him. Fr. Zosima begged whoever it was to stop in the name of Christ and heard in reply, "Father Zosima, forgive me for the Lord's sake. I can-

the typical assumption is that they are historically valid. Therefore, Christ was white, as were the pharaohs, the Egyptians, the prophets and all the peoples in Jerusalem. The description of Jerusalem in Acts 2 gives us a very different image:

> And there were dwelling at Jerusalem, Jews, devout men, out of every nation under heaven. . . . Now when this was noised abroad, the multitude came together, and were confounded, because that every man heard them speak in his own language. . . . Parthians, and Medes, and Elamites, and the dwellers in Mesopotamia, and in Judaea, and Cappadocia, in Pontus, and Asia, Phrygia, and Pamphylia, in Egypt, and in the parts of Libya about Cyrene, and strangers of Rome, Jews and proselytes, Cretes and Arabians, we do hear them speak in our tongues the wonderful works of God. (Acts 2:5, 6, 9-11)

In the time of Christ, Jerusalem was at the center of world trade and commerce. Its strategic location made it a hub through which the peoples of many nations came to conduct their affairs. The Apostles dispersed in each direction, spreading Christianity into Europe, Asia, Asia Minor and Africa. I believe that this was by divine design, that all people might be touched by the Good News of Christ's Holy Resurrection and saving Grace.

It is ironic to me that many ethnic Orthodox churches are located in what are now black neighborhoods. The original Greek, Russian, Romanian, and Ukrainian occupants have long since moved to the suburbs, returning on Sundays only until they can afford to build a new church closer to home. The present residents of those old neighborhoods have no idea of the rich treasure and spiritual wealth that is concealed within those Orthodox Church walls. And the church members have no idea of the great treasure to be harvested in those souls most providentially placed about them. This seems contrary to the spirit of Pentecost and the attitude of the early saints, apostles, fathers and mothers of the Church.

There are those who believe that Orthodoxy is only for Greeks, Serbs, Russians, or other of the historically Orthodox. Unfortunately, the belief that Christianity is a white man's religion persists not only among Black Muslims and misinformed black youth, but in the hearts of those in the Church who should be spreading the Good News and seeking out the sheep that are lost. Ultimately, it is the Holy Spirit that brings souls to the Church, and translates one's attempts at outreach into another's "own tongue." However, the lives of the saints, of every race and nation, offer an aid to dialogue, and a reminder that we have a great witness and source of inspiration very near to us.

# 3

# AFRICAN MONASTICISM: ITS INFLUENCE ON THE REST OF THE WORLD

## FR. PAISIUS ALTSCHUL

**Introduction**

Before our conversion to Orthodoxy, at Reconciliation Ministries in Kansas City, Missouri, we had a men's discipleship house. Men from the city jail, those who were recovering from drugs or alcohol, and others, who were homeless, would come here to live and learn about Christ. During this period I began to read *The Sayings of the Desert Fathers*.[1] I was moved by many of these stories and sayings, but especially by the life of St. Moses the Black. Here was a former murderer, gang leader and thief who had become a desert father. He was not only able to attain a state of dispassion, but was also able to lead many others into this very way of life. What struck me the most was the impact that monasticism had on the formation of his soul and his deliverance from the passions that had controlled him. Here I saw hope for transformation of the lives of the men with whom we were working.

After that introduction to the Desert Fathers of the African Thebaid, I later came across a book called *The Northern Thebaid*.[2] This was a compilation of the lives of Russian desert dwellers who patterned their spiritual struggle on monastic principles that had been developed in ancient Egypt. It was through this particular book that I came in contact with the St. Herman of Alaska Brotherhood, which published it. After meeting my future godfather, Hieromonk

Gerasim, of that Brotherhood, our entire community was led into the Orthodox Church.

We have reaped rich spiritual rewards from the study of the ancient African Fathers and Mothers of the Church. We have found, as well, that their influence was pervasive throughout the ancient Church, and integral to the development of Christianity worldwide, to the present day. In this article, I will identify the sources of ancient African monasticism and trace the path of its influence to the farthest corners of the Christian world.

## Purity of Heart

St. Moses, living in Sketis in Northern Egypt, was once approached by two Europeans seeking to find the purpose for monastic life. He asked them why they had left everything to embrace a life among such rude and uncultured people. They replied that they did so for the Kingdom of Heaven, but they didn't know how monasticism would help them achieve their aim of reaching the Kingdom. To their question as to the purpose of monasticism, St. Moses replied,

> Its immediate purpose . . . is purity of heart, for without this we cannot reach our goal. We should therefore always have this purpose in mind; and, should it ever happen that for a short time our heart turns aside from the direct path, we must bring it back again at once, guiding our lives with reference to our purpose as if it were a carpenter's rule.[3]

This purity of heart—the essential goal of monasticism—has been called by the Fathers a state of dispassion, stillness of soul. The monk becomes a mirror that is clean and that can reflect God and His life to other people. For this purpose the desert Fathers and Mothers embarked on the monastic journey—to bring about stillness to their inner being and share in the glory of God.

## Beginnings of African Monasticism

Let us examine three profiles given by early Christian leaders of the monks in Egypt, in order to get a sense of African monasticism in its own day.

### St. Basil the Great

> I hear that in Egypt at the present time there is virtue of such kind among men, and perhaps there are also some in Palestine living suc-

cessfully the life based on the Gospel. We however are children, certainly in comparison with the perfect. . . . Among us this is rare, since the people are still being instructed in the first principles and introduced to the practice of piety.[4]

### St. John Chrysostom

Commenting on the verse, "Take the young child and his mother, and flee into Egypt" (Mt. 2:13), St. John Chrysostom wrote about Egypt:

> The mother of poets and wise men and magicians, the inventor of every kind of sorcery, but now taking pride in the fishermen and protecting herself with the cross; and not in the cities only, but in the desert even more than in the cities, since everywhere in that land may be seen the camp of Christ. Heaven is not more glorious with its encampment of shining stars than the wilderness of Egypt, studded with the tents of the monks.[5]

### Rufinus

> I have seen, really seen, the treasury of Christ, concealed in human vessels! . . . Yes, I saw in Egypt fathers who lived on the earth, but who led lives in heaven, and certain new prophets, inspired by virtues of the soul, and also the gift of prophecy, whose worthiness was attested to by gifts of signs and wonders . . . some of them were so free of any thought of vice that they had forgotten that there was any evil in the world. . . .[6]

Something occurred in Africa that was so deep, so powerful, and so rich that it affected the rest of the world. Even before the early Christian era, when monasticism flowered, there were spiritual currents that laid the foundations for it. In the Old Testament we see the forerunners of this desert monasticism. Holy ones like Elijah, Elisha, and the school of the prophets (3 and 4 Kings, LXX, 1 and 2 Kings, AV) were living this kind of life in the deserts of Israel. During the inter-testament period we know of the Essene communities that maintained purity, monastic discipline and prophetic expectancy in the desert. This led right up to the Forerunner and Baptist of our Lord Jesus Christ, John, who ate locusts and honey, and was clothed in camel skins, withering the passions for himself and Israel in the desert of Judaea.

As a result of the proclamation of the Good News preached by John, our Lord Jesus Christ and His apostles, and as a result of Christ's death, burial, resurrection and ascension, demonic hosts were confronted and overcome. Swift opposition followed in the form of martyrdoms. This was as our Lord had prophesied, "You shall receive power after that the Holy Spirit has come upon you, and you shall be my witnesses." (Acts 1:8) "Witnesses" is translated from the Greek *martyros* and conveys the idea of so testifying by one's life and words to the message of Christ that the life itself is forfeit. And so it happened. The first three hundred years of the Church comprised the catacomb period. Tertullian, an African leader in third century Carthage, said, "The blood of the martyrs is the seed of the Church."

When the outward, legal persecutions ceased in the beginning of the fourth century, something took place in the hearts of the followers of Christ. They knew that although the external opposition had stopped, they were still engaged in *spiritual* warfare: the demonic hosts had not gone anywhere. Christians were aware of the presence of an invisible plane in which they had daily to deal with very real persecution, even though it was spiritual rather than physical. As a result, people began to leave the cities to face themselves, the demons and God. Trusting in the power of Christ, they withdrew to pray, fast and engage in spiritual combat.

This movement to the desert spread as more and more people began to hear about St. Anthony (251-356 A.D.) and his spiritual exploits in the inner desert. Anthony himself thought he was the only one living this kind of hermitic life. Through revelation he was later to discover St. Paul of Thebes, who had been living this way for ninety years when he met him. There had been others, but none carried the call of the desert as did St. Anthony, whose life was recorded by Patriarch Athanasius of Alexandria, and widely known.

People began to flock to him. He established a way of life for the brothers in which they would continue to live as hermits yet under his guidance as an "abba," a spiritual father. They lived in caves similar to nomads in tents, drawing on God's grace as they sought to pray, fast, work with their hands, recite the Psalms of David and purify their hearts.

On the Western side of the Nile, between present-day Cairo and Alexandria, St. Macarius was shown a valley of natron (native sodium carbonate), called *Wadi Natron,* whose expansive desert spread out to the horizon. It was later called Sketis (Coptic: *shiheet,* i.e., balance of hearts). When the Holy Family had fled from King Herod to Africa 300 years earlier, the Mother of God extended her hand to this region, prophesying that it would be filled with those who would serve her Son to the end of time. To this day it is still a bastion of monasticism and a living testimony to the life of the Desert Fathers.

The "Skete life" is often referred to as the middle form of ascetic life, meaning that it was in between the extremely arduous, and often spiritually dangerous way of life of the hermits on the one hand, and the large structured communities, referred to as coenobitic monasticism, on the other. Skete life was normally a group of monks, all of whom lived "a stone's throw" from each other, gathered around a spiritual father. They would come together on Saturday and Sunday for "Synaxis," i.e., the all-night vigil and Divine Liturgy in commemoration of the Resurrection of Christ. Afterwards they would be able to draw spiritual encouragement from the experiences and counsel of the other brothers. The rest of the week would be spent in prayer and working with one's hands, similarly to the hermits.

Sketis is the place where, we read, St. Moses the Black confessed his sins to St. Macarius and grew under the guidance of St. Isidore; where he and six others were later martyred by the barbarians. This is where St. Paisius the Great (Coptic: St. Bishoy) struggled with his community to serve Christ, and where he was permitted to wash the feet of the Lord. In this region St. John the Dwarf brought forth a monastic community and rescued Thais from a life of harlotry. Thousands of holy ones purified themselves in this very desert. Many of the sayings and lives of the Desert Fathers spring from Sketis. People went to this "place of balance" first to have their hearts weighed in the balance and see their sins, and then, hopefully, to emerge with inward balance of heart and peace of soul.

The third kind of monasticism, the coenobitic life, was developed by St. Pachomius in Upper Egypt. This refers to the area much farther south along the Nile near Tabennesi, near Luxor and Thebes. St. Pachomius was born in 292 A.D. He began his ascetic life as a hermit. Later an angel, clothed as a monk, gave him his monastic rule. As Professor I. M. Kontzevitch says,

> He realized that the solitary way of life was too difficult for novices and did not benefit them. One had to be gradually brought up and prepared to embrace the creative freedom of anchorites (hermits).[7]

It was a strict but very fruitful way of life for tens of thousands of monks and nuns along the Nile. Nine monasteries were developed in this area, including at least one for nuns. They all looked to St. Pachomius as the abbot, the spiritual father.

Whether the monasticism was hermitic, skete, or coenobitic, those seeking the monastic path had left the world to seek God. As a result of this kind of spiritual life, they were able to maintain the "martyr's edge"—that condition of heart which was present during the catacomb period. It was not uncommon for these African deserts to miraculously bring forth springs and begin to vegetate—surely this was a reflection of the action of the Holy Spirit in the lives of the righteous ones who lived there. As these holy ones purified their hearts, they purified their nations and their land. Lay people began to hear about this spiritual dynamism and transformation and, desirous of connecting to these life-giving streams, began to make pilgrimages to these communities.

## The Influence of the Life of St. Anthony

The apostolic patriarch, St. Athanasius of Alexandria, was a friend of St. Anthony of Egypt. St. Anthony was a source of strength and inspiration for him. St. Athanasius authored *The Life of St. Anthony,* the success of which was immediate and far-reaching. One key person that it touched was Blessed Augustine, the future bishop of Hippo (in present day Algeria). The following is from his *Confessions:*

> When then I had told him [Alypius, one Pontitianus, our countryman so far as being an African, in high office in the Emperor's court . . .] that I bestowed very great pains upon those Scriptures, a conversation arose (suggested by his account) on Anthony the Egyptian Monk: whose name was in high reputation among Thy servants, though to that hour unknown to us. Which when he discovered, he dwelt the more upon that subject, informing and wondering at our ignorance of one so eminent.[8]

In this next passage we find his own inspiration for seeking guidance for monastic life coming again from the life of St. Anthony.

> So checking the torrent of my tears, I arose; interpreting it to be no other than a command from God to open the book and read the first chapter I should find. For I heard of Anthony, that coming in during the reading of the Gospel, he received the admonition, as if what was being read, was spoken to him: Go, sell all that thou hast, and give to the poor, and thou shalt have treasure in heaven, and come and follow me. And by such oracle he was forthwith converted unto Thee.[9]

## Jerome on Anthony and Serapion

Blessed Jerome (†420 A.D.), a prolific writer among the Western Fathers, writes:

> Anthony the monk, whose life Athanasius of Alexandria wrote a long work upon, sent seven letters in Coptic to various monasteries, letters truly apostolic in idea and language, and which have been translated

into Greek. The chief of these is *To the Arsenoites*. He flourished during the reign of Constantius and his sons.[10]

In another place, he describes the initial African monastics:

> I will pass on, therefore, to the third class, called anchorites, who go from the monasteries into the deserts, with nothing but bread and salt. Paul [of Thebes, the hermit] introduced this way of life; Anthony made it famous, and—to go farther back still—John the Baptist set the first example of it.[11]

## African Monastic Influence on Women Monastics

Blessed Jerome also provides insight on the spread of African monasticism among the women in Rome. He brought to light for the West what was rapidly spreading throughout Africa and the East. Prior to this period, for a woman to be a nun was considered strange and degrading. But due to the enlightenment of SS. Athanasius and Peter of Alexandria, the beauty of women's monasticism was made known. When they had fled to Rome for protection from the persecution of the Arian heretics, the saints described the hermitic life of St. Anthony and the communities established by Saint Pachomius in the South in the Thebaid. A certain Marcella, hearing about the life established for the virgins and widows by St. Pachomius, decided to take up the easy yoke of Christ in the monastic life. Years later she was followed by Sophronia, and then by others. In Blessed Jerome's own words:

> My revered friend Paula was blessed with Marcella's friendship, and it was in Marcella's cell that Eustochium, that paragon of virgins, was gradually trained. Thus it is easy to see, of what type the mistress was who found such pupils. . . . For we judge of people's virtue not by their sex but by their character, and hold those to be worthy of the highest glory who have renounced both rank and wealth.[12]

## Gennadius

Gennadius (†480 A.D.), a disciple of Blessed Jerome, provides brief profiles of some of the key African monastic leaders of his period. This is but one of many collections of the lives and sayings of the Desert Fathers that were to become so influential in the spread of monasticism and thereby deepen the moral fabric of the Church.

He gives brief sketches of St. Pachomius and of his successor, Theodore. He describes Oresiesis the monk, the co-struggler of both Pachomius and Theodore, a man who "learned to perfection in Scripture, composed a book seasoned with divine salt and formed of the essentials of all monastic discipline," and Macarius of Egypt, "distinguished for his miracles and virtues" as well as his writings. We also learn of Evagrius the monk, a disciple of Macarius, who "wrote many things of use to monks." Gennadius describes St. John Cassian, called "the Roman," a "Scythian by race, ordained deacon by Bishop John the Great [Chrysostom], at Constantinople." A priest at Marseilles, St. John Cassian established two monasteries, one for men and one for women. Gennadius refers to his writing of the influential "*Conferences* with the Egyptian fathers."[13]

Gennadius was an early and important witness to the enormous influence of the sayings and lives of the holy African Desert Fathers.

## African Monastic Influence on Western Europe

Fr. Seraphim Rose, a modern day American monk who modeled his way of life on this African desert tradition, speaks both from his writings and experience. In *Vita Patrum*,[14] he highlights the African roots of the monastic movement that flowered in Gaul (now France) and the rest of Western Europe. In his introduction to the lives of the ancient French monastic saints, he relates:

> The lands of the West, from Italy to Britain, knew both the preaching of the Apostles and the deeds of the martyrs; here the Christian seed was planted so firmly that the West responded immediately and enthusiastically when it heard of the great ascetics of Egypt and the East. St. Athanasius' *Life* of St. Anthony the Great was quickly translated into Latin, and the best of the sons and daughters of the West went to the East to learn from the great Fathers there. . . . St. John Cassian the Roman learned so thoroughly the spiritual doctrine of the Egyptian Fathers that his books (the *Institutes* and *Conferences*) became the chief foundation of the authentic monastic tradition of the West. The great seedbed of Orthodox monasticism in 5th century Gaul—Lerins—grew up entirely under the influence of the Eastern monastic tradition.[15]

Fr. Seraphim goes on to show that when the life of the Egyptian ascetics was lived and practiced elsewhere, the basic results remained the same. As souls were transformed in Africa, so now in Europe. St. Martin of Tours, inspired by *The Life of St. Anthony*, lived according to the desert ideal. His miraculous life was recorded by his disciple, and as St. Anthony had inspired St. Martin, so now St. Martin inspired others.

St. Martin was a key transmitter of the way of life that had come from the African monks:

That he had an impact on his times and that a large part of that impact was monastic in the Egyptian ascetical mode, we can judge from the historic results. An Egyptian form of monasticism flourished in Tours, which combined the Eremitic [hermit type] with the coenobitic life. And the fame of Martin's life and miracles, spread first by Severus (†c. 420), then by St. Gregory of Tours (†594) and finally by Venantius Fortunatus (†600) is solidly connected by all three with the introduction and development of this monastic tradition. Further, Western monks looked to Martin as an exemplar, and many monasteries were named after and dedicated to him.[16]

Thus, the monastic ideal spread. Again and again, we see that the spiritual rivers that sustained European Christians flowed from African headwaters.

African Christian spirituality also came to the West through St. Benedict and the Benedictines, perhaps the most widely known Western monastic community. In St. Benedict's rule for the monks, he commends the writings of St. John Cassian and the sayings of the Desert Fathers, demonstrating once again the African origins of their monasticism.

## St. John Cassian

St. John Cassian is one of the most important bridges between African and European monasticism. He and his co-struggler Germanus spent time with the African Desert Fathers, living their life, praying with them, and recording their teaching. A tremendous debt is owed to these African monks who passed on to St. John the oral teaching that he so faithfully committed to writing. In the *Institutes,* which described the rules and customs of Egyptian monastic practice, he recorded the means for combating the eight vices that the Fathers saw as most destructive. The *Conferences* were interviews with the best known of the Desert Fathers, especially those in Sketis, such as St. Moses.

Fr. Seraphim Rose points out that in the early days, among the disciples of St. Martin of Tours and the other French monastic strugglers, there was little material available for spiritual direction outside of Athanasius' *Life of St. Anthony,* and some early Latin copies of the *Lives and Sayings of the Desert Fathers.* While St. Martin was alive, that was sufficient, since his personal influence was so keenly felt. But after his repose, as the French monks grew into the thousands,

the need for a rather "systematic" written account of the monastic teaching became acutely felt. As with one voice, the monastic fathers of Gaul turned for this account to St. John Cassian, abbot of a newly founded monastery in Marseilles, who had just returned from long sojourn in the monastic deserts of Egypt and Palestine. Having thoroughly absorbed the teaching of the Eastern Fathers, and being a man of spiritual discernment himself, he answered their pleas with two books: the *Institutes . . .* and *the Conferences.*[17]

Fr. Seraphim here draws attention to the fact that the formative books of hermits in the mountains of Gaul were the *Institutes* of St. John Cassian and the *Lives* of the African Desert Fathers:

> It is above all the *Institutes* that set the tone for monasticism of this period. St. Gregory of Tours himself, when he had occasion to give spiritual instruction to a recluse of his diocese, "sent him books with the lives of the Fathers and the Institutes of the Monks, so that he might learn what recluses ought to be and with what prudence monks ought to behave. When he had read and re-read them, not only did he drive out of his mind bad thoughts which he had had, but even more it so developed his knowledge that he astonished us with his facility in speaking of these matters." (*Life of the Fathers,* 20:3) These same two books are the ones that St. Romanus took with him when he set out for his hermit's life in the Jura Mountains. But even apart from its direct influence on monastic aspirants, the *Institutes* may be seen also clearly reflected in the teaching of the monastic Fathers of Gaul who came after him.[18]

What was the aim of this spiritual literature being generated through contact with the blossoming African desert monasticism? Fr. Seraphim Rose, who imbibed deeply of this tradition, and bravely claimed his own "Thebaid" in the wilderness of Northern California, tells us:

> The purpose of the monastic discipline is to uproot the passions and acquire the virtues. In Egypt, the elders see that novices "discover both the causes of the passions by which they are tempted, and the means against them. . . . These true physicians of souls, averting by spiritual instruction as by some heavenly medicine the afflictions of heart that might arise in the future, do not allow the passions to grow in the souls of youths, revealing to them both the cause of the passion that threatens, and the means for healing" (XI: 16). It may well be imagined what pain this self-knowledge causes to the soul of the novice, who usually comes to a monastery full of illusion about himself.[19]

## African Influence in Celtic and British Spirituality

We have already seen that the monastic life in Gaul was deeply influenced by African monasticism. Few realize that the teacher of St.

Patrick, St. Germanus of Auxerre, passed on to him this same Gallic spirituality.

> When Patrick was thirty years old [approx. 420 A.D.] . . . he crossed the southern British sea and began his journey through Gaul. . . . He came to the home of a very holy bishop, Germanus, who ruled the city of Auxerre, the greatest lord in almost all of Gaul. Patrick stayed with him for quite some time, just as Paul sat at the feet of Gamaliel. In all humility, patience, and obedience he learned, loved, and treasured wholeheartedly knowledge, wisdom, purity, and every benefit to soul and spirit, with great fear and love for God, in goodness and singleness of heart and chaste in body and spirit.[20]

The *Life of St. Anthony* also reached Northern England. Both St. Anthony and St. Benedict were referred to by St. Cuthbert's biographer.[21] The patron saint of Wales, David, looked to the monks of Egypt for his example and instituted their practices in his monasteries.

Late in the seventh century, Adrian, a black monk, came to England from Italy, having served in a monastery near Naples, and inspired a tremendous flourishing of monasticism. His scholarship and devotion had long been recognized and his teaching skills and sanctity were most evident to his former superiors. In 670 A.D., Pope Vitalian wanted to consecrate him as Archbishop of Canterbury. But Adrian was a humble man and replied to the pope that he felt unworthy to take on such an important assignment. Instead he urged that the pope appoint another man who was as scholarly and dedicated as he. This was St. Theodore of Tarsus. The pope agreed on the condition that St. Adrian would go along as St. Theodore's spiritual father and advisor.

St. Theodore proved to an able administrator and built the operational structure of the Church of England, with St. Adrian's constant advice and support. St. Adrian was appointed Abbot at the monastery of SS. Peter and Paul at Canterbury. For thirty years he taught the monks, priests, and lay people to understand the Scriptures. He also trained the priests in Latin and Greek. St. Adrian was a priceless asset to the Church.

### African Monasticism in Palestine

The rivers of African desert sanctity flowed not only into Europe, but into nearby Palestine as well. From the time of St. Anthony, monasticism in Palestine could be considered the daughter of monasticism in Africa. For instance, one of the disciples of St. Anthony, St. Hilarion, left Egypt for Palestine to pursue the spiritual life near Gaza. Later other hermits began to gather around him. Building on this, Epiphanias established another monastery nearby. Later, lavras (larger monastic communities) began to emerge. Professor Kontzevitch provides an overview of Palestine's development from this point:

> The first lavra, Faran, was cared for by St. Chariton near Jerusalem. Ten other lavras sprang up along the way from Jerusalem to Jericho, and around Bethlehem. St. Euthymius established his monastery in the 5th century, and in the 6th century St. Sabbas the Sanctified founded his monastery with a lenient community rule, where life in a community was regarded as a preliminary step towards going out to live an individual life as a hermit.[22]

There was another African influence in Palestine in the sixth century. St. Barsanuphius was born in Egypt and was learned in both the Egyptian and Greek languages. He traveled to the monastery of Abba Seridos in Gaza and lived and labored there in solitude. St. Barsanuphius and his disciple St. John became renowned as clairvoyant elders full of the gifts of the Holy Spirit, and many turned to them for spiritual counsel. They left a book of questions and answers on the spiritual life which has been relied on by monastics throughout the world ever since.[23]

## Muslim Invasions

African Christianity was already firmly established six hundred years before Mohammed. African monasticism was at its height three hundred years before him. To state that Islam is the natural religion of the African is a denial of history. With its militaristic emphasis, Islam forced many of the African Christians back into the catacombs. The ruler of Egypt, Abiza, banned people from becoming monastics, by threat of torture. The monastic life had to find other outlets of expression. Constantinople and Mt. Athos in the north and Ethiopia in the south became places of continued monastic development. Constantinople was said to have become like "a monastic kingdom." All three types of monasticism flourished in these regions. The monastic rules of St. Pachomius and St. Basil the Great were followed and became the foundation of other rules developed during this period.

## Hesychasm Rooted in African Monasticism

The ideas of stillness of soul and constant prayer in the heart are an integral part of Eastern Christian spirituality. They are known by the term *hesychasm* (i.e., *hesychia*—stillness) and are associated with the monastic way of life. The three stages of the method of hesychasm are first, *purification* of sins and passions; second, *illumination,* when unceasing prayer and watchfulness occur in the heart; and third, *deification,* when one partakes of the glory of God. Although all Orthodox Christians are called to hesychasm, the monastics have been the faithful guardians and transmitters of the hesychastic tradition. In the early Byzantine period, hesychasm denoted the ascetic endeavors of a solitary desert-dweller, a hermit. In the later Byzantine period, it was used in reference to monks who devoted themselves to absolute silence, holy repose, inner spiritual concentration and unceasing "mental" prayer. These disciplines eventually led to a particular state of blessedness, to the vision of uncreated light similar to the light that surrounded Christ on Mt. Tabor. Hesychasm reached its height during the fourteenth century.

Ancient African asceticism contributed greatly toward the emergence of this still vital spiritual tradition. Hierarch Porphyrius Uspensky found in the libraries of Mt. Athos tenth- to fifteenth-century anthologies with selections from ancient lives of the Holy Fathers about prayer and inward activity.[24] This discovery indicated that the sources of hesychasm could be found in the early centuries of the Church. St. Anthony, in the third century, spoke of stillness: "Let us be men of silence and hesychasts." He instructed Blessed Theodora on the necessity of becoming quiet and keeping silence, of sitting in her cell and recollecting the mind within herself. Blessed Theodora said: "Rest from cares, silence and innermost soaring of the mind constitute unceasing prayer: Lord Jesus Christ, Son of God, help me." This is a very early reference to what came to be known as The Jesus Prayer. This prayer is often mentioned in the *Paradise of the Holy Fathers*[25] and other anthologies.

St. Macarius was one of the first hesychasts. As Archimandrite Cyprian writes,

> . . . from his mystical experience St. Macarius knew what path all Eastern mysticism would subsequently take. His instructions on the struggle with the passions, on the purification of the heart, on freeing the mind, *i.e.* on its sobriety, all pursue the main objective: man's illumination. The mystical teaching of light, which is attained by quieting the mind from everything that may disturb and exasperate it, was well known to this desert dweller of the 4th century, one thousand years

before St. Gregory Palamas and the hesychasts came out with their teaching on the subject. Their very term "hesychia" (stillness) was frequently used by him in association with the concepts of "peace," "calming down," "prayer," "silence," etc. Hesychasm was in no way an "innovation" or "invention." St. Gregory of Sinai gave an even clearer and more precise definition of what the ascetics of the 4th century knew from experience.[26]

From Africa to Greece to the Slavic countries, the African monastic stream moved forward. Professor Kontzevitch traces this development in Bulgaria and then Russia. In Bulgaria, we find that *The Life of St. Anthony* was translated in the ninth century during the golden age of Bulgarian literature. The founder of Russian monasticism, St. Anthony of the Kiev Caves Lavra [†1073], was tonsured on Mt. Athos. St. Nestor, the chronicler of the Kiev Caves saints, reflected that St. Anthony of the Kiev Caves was glorified like Anthony of Egypt. What St. Anthony of Egypt was to African monasticism, St. Anthony of Kiev became to Russian monasticism—the spiritual father and fountainhead.

## African Influence and the Philokalia

Due in large part to the references to *The Philokalia* in the recently popular *The Way of a Pilgrim,* many modern readers have begun to rediscover these ancient texts. Yet few realize how deeply embedded they are in African spirituality.

*The Philokalia* is a spiritual anthology written between the fourth and the fifteenth centuries by spiritual masters of the Orthodox tradition. In Greek, the word *philokalia* means "lover of beauty," i.e., the true spiritual beauty that comes from experiencing the goodness of God from a pure heart. As a collection, it was first published in Greek in 1782, translated into Slavonic and later into Russian. *The Philokalia* has exercised an enormous influence on the recent history of the Orthodox Church:

> . . . Indeed the impact of the *Philokalia* on Russian spirituality and culture in the nineteenth century was immense, as the writings of Dostoevsky, an assiduous reader of the book, alone sufficiently testify. A translation into Russian was made by Ignatius Brianchaninov (1807-1867) and was published in 1857. Yet another Russian translation, still with the title *Dobrotolubiye,* was made by Bishop Theophan the Recluse (1815-1894).[27]

Even a cursory examination of *The Philokalia* reveals that the work is dominated by the writings of the African Fathers and those who were influenced by them. St. Anthony of Egypt, St. Macarius the Great, St. Mark the Ascetic, Evagrius of Pontus, St. John Cassian, and St. Moses the Ethiopian are just a few of those included in one of the most important spiritual treasuries of the Christian world.

## St. Seraphim and the African Fathers

The effect that African monasticism has had on the formation of spiritual life throughout the world is indeed remarkable. Even in our contemporary period, these waters have not run dry. In nineteenth-century Russia, the influence of St. Paisius Velichkovsky and his disciples, living by the wisdom of *The Philokalia,* resulted in a revival of monastic life of the kind that had flourished in ancient Africa. To describe the effects of this spiritual dynamic, let us consider the same phenomenon in both the Russian forests and the Egyptian deserts. St. Anthony of Siya, in his cell in what has been called the "Northern Thebaid" of Russia, lived in a cave covered with snow from which he lifted up holy prayers with warm tears. St. Paul of Obnora lived for three years in the hollow of a linden tree. Without the supernatural assistance of God, one winter alone would have been enough to cause his death. When St. Seraphim of Sarov, his body covered with snow, was before the eyes of his disciple Motovilov transfigured with uncreated light and warmth, he described this as "acquiring the Holy Spirit." He told him:

> No pleasantness of earthly fragrance can be compared with the fragrance which we now smell, for we are surrounded by the fragrance of the Holy Spirit. Notice, your God-love, how you told me that around us it is as warm as a bath; but look, neither on you nor on me does the snow melt, nor above us either. Therefore, this warmth is not in the air, but in us. This is that very warmth of which the Holy Spirit, in the words of the prayer, causes us to cry out to the Lord: "Warm me with the warmth of Thy Holy Spirit." Being warmed by it, men and women desert-dwellers did not fear the winter frost, being clothed as in warm fur coats in a garment of grace woven by the Holy Spirit.

These words refer to the Russian ascetics. But in the Egyptian desert the picture was different and the nature of the manifestation of help from Above was different also.[28] In Egypt we discover St. Onuphrius living in the sand dunes, offering his life as incense before God. St. Paphnutius relates how he was supernaturally sustained there by palm branches that bore dates each month; how holy angels nourished him with Holy Communion; how water fountains suddenly sprang forth to bring healing and refreshment. As Professor Kontzevitch explains,

> These anchorites, as also later Russian anchorites, following their example, for the sake of God renounced everything that belongs to human nature, all the way to the instinct of self-preservation, and threw themselves into the abyss of God's mercy unconditionally, preserving only the faith which moves mountains. And this faith, in both Russia and Egypt, proved to be justified.[29]

St. Onuphrius and most of the other African Desert Fathers lived in the fourth and fifth centuries. St. Seraphim lived a little more than a hundred years ago. Although separated by fifteen hundred years, the spiritual phenomenon is the same. The desert ideal is a spiritual reality that is being pursued to this very day. Again, Professor Kontzevitch reflects:

> This is not some mysterious remote antiquity in the mist of the ages. But it is precisely now, when our spiritual wings have become atrophied and we have forgotten what possibilities are concealed in our spirit, that St. Seraphim was sent to us, in all the power and spiritual might of the Ancient Fathers, so that we might remember our divine sonship and strive towards the limitless perfection of our Heavenly Father.[30]

The truly marvelous thing is that this grace and activity of the Holy Spirit within the monastic communities of Africa and Russia is still available to us. St. Seraphim did not claim that his "Wonderful Revelation to the World" was anything new or unique, only that it had been lost. Those who have read the homilies of St. Macarius the Great of Egypt will find St. Seraphim's teachings to be very familiar. St. Seraphim often uses the very same words, images and parables as St. Macarius to describe the need to acquire the Holy Spirit. Both use the Gospel parable of the ten virgins in the same way, describing the oil that was needed for the lamps as the "grace of the Spirit from above" and explaining that "the acquisition of the Holy Spirit is, so to say, the oil that the virgins lacked."[31] The similarity is striking. The important point is not whether St. Seraphim knew the homilies of St. Macarius the Great, but rather, that both saints were partakers of the same tradition and imbued with the same Holy Spirit.

## Conclusion

The ultimate source of the spirituality we have been discussing is not Africa, or Palestine, or Russia. It is the Holy Trinity. As the Lord Jesus Christ said, "He that believes in Me, out of his innermost being shall flow rivers of living water." (Jn. 7:37) Nevertheless, it is only right to "give honor where honor is due" (Rom. 13:7), and again, to "remember those that led you, who spoke the Word of God to you, and considering the outcome of their life, imitate their faith." (Heb. 13:7) For too long, little or no honor has been paid to those who have laid the foundations in Africa for the preservation of Christianity throughout the world. Historically, African monastics, and later, monastics everywhere, have acted as the salt of the earth holding back the corruption of the world. I have shown that the roots and headwaters for this monastic flourishing had their source in African soil. Unfortunately, black saints have been depicted as white and African bishops have been portrayed as Europeans. The remembrance and acknowledgment of our historic spiritual foundations is long overdue. Perhaps as more and more Africans and African-Americans in the Western Diaspora consider ancient Orthodox Christianity, they will be able to see it for what it is: the Faith, from a people of color, to be shared with all the world, where "There is neither Jew nor Greek; slave or freeman; male or female; for you are all one in Christ Jesus." (Gal. 3:28)

I believe that hope for solutions to our current dilemmas can be drawn from the African monastic influence. One of the great African monastic fathers, St. Mark the Ascetic, wrote, "Remembrance of God is pain of heart, endured in a spirit of devotion. But he who forgets God becomes self-indulgent, and thereby, insensitive."

During the time of Catacomb Christianity, remembrance of God was very near for the martyrs. Their pain of heart, endured with a longing love for God, produced a spiritual union indescribable to those outside the faith. Many that suffered the horrors of slavery and the resulting American Apartheid had an experience similar to that of the early Christian martyrs. Some of these African-American slaves were also martyred, as well as subjected to every kind of torture, because of their faith and devotion to Jesus Christ. With this suffering came an amazing legacy of spiritual depth like that of the ancient Catacomb Christians.

Yet as Christianity in the fourth century grew in acceptance by the established world system, with a corresponding cooling of zeal for Christ, so today, as strides toward civil progress are realized (ever so slowly), there is developing this same cooling of zeal. The answer then was not a return to legal persecution so as to promote spiritual depth; and it is the same today, when all steps toward justice and true liberty are to be encouraged. However, as then, whole hosts of spiritual warriors in the Egyptian deserts sought to maintain their martyr's edge by facing God, themselves and the demons, so now, the desert is waiting. For some, the desert might be the monastic experience in the wilderness, as sought by Fr. Seraphim Rose and others at St. Herman of Alaska Monastery in Northern California. For others, the desert might be the inner city, where like-minded strugglers gather together to live an ascetic life. In both deserts, we must face God, ourselves, and the demons. We must seek to purify our hearts, acquire peace and the grace of the Holy Spirit.

At great personal price, the spiritual Fathers and Mothers of Africa laid the foundations for monastic life throughout the world. The teaching and examples of those holy ones provide us with answers on how to be transformed in this present generation. New exploits await the future spiritual fathers and mothers of Africa. Surrounded by pleasures, passions, quick fixes and cheap substitutes that ultimately backfire, the modern soul longs for what is real, what works, and what connects us to eternity and the other world. May we draw from those African rivers of ancient wisdom and be transformed ourselves. As St. Seraphim of Sarov said, "Acquire inward peace and thousands around you will be saved."

# 4

# ETHIOPIA STRETCHES OUT HER HANDS TO GOD

## FR. DEACON KINFU DIBAWO

ETHIOPIA! ETHIOPIA IS AN ANCIENT LAND, whose origins date back thousands of years before the birth of Jesus Christ. From about the time of King Solomon of Israel, the nation of Ethiopia worshipped one God, the God of our fathers, Abraham, Isaac, and Jacob. This makes Ethiopia a unique country, not only on the continent of Africa, but also in the whole world, as it is the only one that converted to Christianity from Judaism, rather than paganism. The following is a brief, personal account of Ethiopia's rich spiritual tradition, which is intimately bound up with her history. I have also included some information on the Ark of the Covenant, essential to an understanding of our culture. A historical overview and summary of the reign of Haile Selassie I, Ethiopia's beloved emperor, compiled by Fr. Paisius Altschul, follows.

### Traditions

Some of the work Ethiopian artisans produced in antiquity is still standing. In Axum, the ancient Ethiopian capital in the North, there is found a 2,000-year-old obelisk, 100 feet high, that was carved out of a single stone. Another ancient work of wonder is the church of St. Giorgis (St. George) in Lalibela. Often depicted on posters of Ethiopia, this massive church was carved out of a single rock in the thirteenth century, bearing the shape of a cross. There are many similar churches and monasteries in Ethiopia that reflect the work of early African Christians.

Historic Ethiopian engravings and carvings reflect both the ancient, and in many cases, what is still, the people's way of life and surroundings. Many different types of wildlife, often reflected in woodwork, still find refuge in Ethiopia. Some are rare species that are not found anywhere else in the world.

Liturgical objects are often forged from brass, silver or gold. Others are carved from wood. Crosses, *macomia* (prayer staffs), *sistrum* (timbrels, or tambourines of an ancient style), and censers are all handcrafted and used in the worship of the Holy Trinity. Elaborately decorated crosses are commonly carried at the front of religious processions. For us, there is a reality to symbols. The Greek word for symbol (*symbolos*) means "to gather together." The opposite of that is *diabolos* (where we get the word "devil") which means "to scatter, to break apart, to cause havoc." We think of the symbols of the Church as a focal point that brings us together and draws our attention to eternal realities. In this sense, when we carry the Cross, we have a symbol of Christ's victory over sin, hell and death, as well as of our freedom—our liberation through Jesus Christ.

The blessing cross is a means whereby the grace of the Holy Spirit is extended to those in need. The Gospel is often depicted in the artwork on the crosses themselves. Customarily, one will find a figure with four sides and three points on each side. The number four represents the four Gospels and the effects of the Cross being taken to the four quarters of the earth. The number three represents the Holy Trinity: the Father, the Son and the Holy Spirit, one God. Christ is depicted being supported by the four Cherubim, as is revealed by the prophet Ezekiel and in the book of Revelation. The Mother of God is often depicted, because she, like the Cherubim, carried God.

Ethiopia was one of the first countries in the world to translate the Hebrew text of the Holy Bible. It was translated into Ge'ez, a Semitic language native to Ethiopia, similar to Hebrew and Arabic. The Ge'ez Scriptures were to be used by the Church and for the education of the people. For hundreds of years, the Church was the only source of education. The Ethiopic alphabet was developed several thousand years ago, and the Ethiopian Church has been able to publish many very ancient manuscripts.

During times of trouble, when the country is plagued with floods, drought, or invasion, there are particular petitions and supplications that are offered all over the nation in places of worship and in private homes. This practice dates back to the kind of petitions that were offered when the Prophet Jonah told the city of Nineveh that in forty days it would be judged. The fervency, the humbling of self, the piety, the heartfelt repentance of these public prayers—all this expresses the moving cry of a people for the mercy of God. These supplications are each said twelve times and are called "*Xyota.*" They are regularly prayed at almost every gathering of Ethiopian Orthodox Christians today.

The Ethiopian *Tewahedo* (i.e., Unity, Oneness, Integration) Orthodox Church has its own unique liturgical melodies, which were composed by St. Yared, after a divine revelation. The Saint composed the entire structure of worship and praises of the Church in accordance with the book of Psalms 150:2-6, which states, "Praise ye the Lord, praise Him with timbrel and dance. Alleluia!" Sung to the accompaniment of the liturgical sistrum (small timbrel), liturgical drums, *macomia* and liturgical dance, the liturgy conveys the reverent feeling of ancient worship in Israel around the Ark of the Covenant.

From Old Testament times to the present, the majority of Ethiopian churches have been built in the shape of a circle, with several concentric walls, leading to the center, where the *tabot* (the Ark), the Holy Gospel, and the Holy Eucharist preside on the altar table. Upon entering the church, one notices that the walls and ceiling are totally covered with frescoes and icons (i.e., sacred pictures depicting Christ, His Mother, the saints, events in the Gospel, etc. that are held in honor by the faithful).

## The Ark of the Covenant

According to the Holy Scriptures, King Solomon had many wives. An ancient text in the Ethiopic tradition, *Kebra Negast* (The Glory of the Kings), reveals the story of King Solomon, the Queen of Sheba, and their child, Menelik I. Menelik embraced the faith of Israel and the worship of the God of Abraham, Isaac and Jacob. He was allowed to bring hundreds of Jewish priests from Israel to establish Judaism in Ethiopia. The priests, according to tradition, secretly brought with them the Ark of the Covenant. Up to this present day, every one of the Ethiopian Orthodox churches has resting on its altar a *tabot,* an ark. Each of these arks contains holy inscriptions from the New Testament which illustrate its connection to the Old Testament Ark. The following is a quote from Fr. Jeremias Gabede Welde Jesus Libreyed on the Ark of the Covenant:

The Ark, until the advent of Christianity, continued to be the powerful source of inspiration and the binding force of unity. Not only in the religious, cultural and social aspects of the lives of the Ethiopians, but also in the fabrics of their economic activities, political setup and national identity. When the sacraments of the Church were instituted [the Orthodox Church has seven sacraments or mysteries], the Ark of the Covenant, which contained the tablets bearing the inscriptions of the Word of God, ceased to be *the* Holy Object of Worship.

When the Word of God, Jesus Christ, became incarnate in fulfillment of the many Bible prophecies, it was revealed that the commission of the Ark of the Covenant (which had been His symbolic precursor), had come to completion. The Ark was made to retire from public use. Since that time it has been kept hidden and sacred, and is commonly considered to be kept in St. Mary's Church in Axum by a holy priest specially selected for this purpose. Again, Fr. Jeremias points out:

> Therefore, the birth of Christ rendered the Ark of the Covenant a Divine Mystery in regards to its existence on earth henceforth. In order to preserve the tradition of its sojourn in Ethiopia, it was historically set aside and placed in a special shrine in Axum, where it is highly revered as a sacred relic and well looked after under a life-time keeper, appointed specifically for this function by the electoral college of Axum Zion. However, a similar object, corresponding to the Ark of the Covenant but fashioned according to the precepts of the New Testament, was instituted in its place in the sanctuary of the transformed Christian Church, dedicated to St. Mary of Zion, the archetype of the Ark of the Covenant.

Here Mary, the Mother of God, is referred to as the archetype of the Ark. She is for us that sacred Ark that carried the Living Word of God. Just as the Old Testament Ark carried the manna, the holy bread that came down from heaven and the Law of the Covenant, so now, Mary, the Mother of God, carried for us Jesus, the Living Bread that came down out of Heaven, as well as the Living Word of God. Thus, she is venerated as the Ark who carried the Living Bread for us. Fr. Jeremias continues:

> The new sacred object in substitute of the tablets of the Old Testament carries the engravings of Jesus Christ, with the images of the Holy Virgin Mary, and John the Disciple, each standing on the right and left sides of the Cross respectively, and with the Divine Names of God inscribed thereon, signifying the incarnation of the Word of God in the womb of St. Mary. The original Ark of the Covenant remained all the time a single, sacred object for the whole message of the Old

Testament books. The first New Testament tablet contained in the new Ark, symbolizing both Christ and His Holy Mother respectively, was produced to be used as an altar, on which the Eucharist, the sacrificial offering of the Body and Blood of Christ, is presented in the Liturgical worship of the Holy Communion with God. Since then, a replica of the New Testament version of the tablet, reproduced in marble or in special wood and contained in the wooden ark (*tabot*), is placed on the altar of every church consecrated to fulfill the Christian sacraments brought about through the salvation of Jesus Christ, born of the Virgin Mary.

When the people of Ethiopia have a problem they gather around the *tabot*. This represents gathering around the New Covenant that God has made with His people. This is truly a *symbolos,* a drawing together. Unfortunately, the importance of symbols is one key thing that has been neglected in most contemporary churches. They have forgotten the significance of honoring the Mother of God and the Holy Ones that went before us, the holy places, and holy objects such as the Ark. As a result, because nothing is considered really sacred, even that which is most sacred to modernists—the Holy Scriptures—are being disregarded. People neglect them, dishonor them and no longer live by them. Once you start to tear apart Holy Things, it's just a matter of time before nothing is holy.

## Conclusion

Ethiopia. She stands for us as a reminder of the Holiness of God. Over and over in the worship services one hears the word, *Kiddus,* meaning Holy. Holiness permeates the cultural and religious life of the Ethiopian people. When they greet each other, Ethiopians bow to show their respect. This bow is given to both men and women to honor them as the image of God. It's a way of regarding others so as to lift them up, to be at their service, to help them. These qualities of humility and charity and service have been developed in the souls of Ethiopians throughout the long history of their nation's carrying the Holy Faith.

Many of her children have been scattered because of the tribulations that have come upon Ethiopia in recent times. In this land of America, many children of Africa, forced here through slavery, have been crying out for help. Ethiopian Orthodox Christians have treasure to share. The idea of Christianity as a "white man's religion" is very foreign to Ethiopian Christians. From King Solomon to His Imperial Majesty, Haile Selassie I, the faith of Africa has been preserved. Now, lest it be hidden under a bushel, let it shine to all in need. Let the waters of the Gihon once again give drink to those thirsty for truth from ancient Africa. In the Name of the Father, and of the Son, and of the Holy Spirit, One God. Amen.

## Ethiopia—A Historical Overview

The richness and scope of Ethiopia's history is reflected in several passages of the Holy Scriptures. In Psalm 68:31, we read: "Ethiopia shall soon stretch out her hands to God." Of the four rivers that God placed to flow into Eden, the second one is named *Gihon.* About this river, we read in the book of Genesis 2:13: "And the name of the second river is Gihon, the same that compasseth the whole land of Ethiopia." In another account from the Holy Scriptures, we learn that God refers to the Ethiopians as His children. In the words of the prophet, it is written, "Are you not as children of Ethiopia unto Me, O children of Israel?" (Amos 9:1) These passages in the Holy Bible reveal that, from ancient times, Ethiopia has been chosen and blessed by God to reveal His Word.

We know of many historic African kings and queens. In Ethiopia alone, from the time that King Solomon was the ruler of Israel until His Imperial Majesty, Haile Selassie I, there have been 334 Kings and Queens. These were direct descendants of King Solomon and Queen Makeda (the "Queen of the South").

King Menelik I brought Judaism to Ethiopia with the Ark of the Covenant. It grew and developed until the time of Jesus Christ. One of the three magi that came to worship Him came from Ethiopia. The Book of Acts states that on the day of Pentecost (the Jewish feast of Shevuoth), as was the custom, Jews were gathered from all the Diaspora. One of these was the Ethiopian eunuch, who is understood to have been a high-ranking finance minister in the court of Queen Candace. When St. Philip found the eunuch reading the prophecies from the scroll of Isaiah, he explained to him about the Messiah, Jesus. Immediately upon hearing this, the Ethiopian emissary was baptized and took the Holy Faith of our Lord Jesus Christ back to Ethiopia.

Nurtured through the efforts of the Holy Apostle Matthew, the Christian faith grew for the next few hundred years. In the fourth century, two young Phoenicians were shipwrecked off the Ethiopian coast. One of these was Frumentius, or Abba Selama. He informed St. Athanasius of Alexandria about the reception of Christianity in Ethiopia. St. Athanasius sent him back, now ordained as bishop, to care for the flock of the Lord and to administer the sacraments. Since that time to this, the Ethiopian Orthodox Church has grown to over 16 million members, with 20,000 churches, 250,000 priests and 857 monasteries. It has produced countless saints and martyrs. St. Yared, St. Tekla Haimanot, St. Gabre Manfes Kiddus are but a very few.

Some of these holy ones have been righteous kings in Ethiopia. Although the kings of Ethiopia were conscious of their power, they always asked for Divine intervention in defending their country. Thus, on the battleground the defenders of the faith and the land were led in procession by the clergy and the *tabot*. Holy icons often decorated the swords of the defenders of the faith that fought against foreign invaders.

Generally, in the Eastern Christian understanding, Christian kings would not seek to conquer other countries in order to extend Christianity (as occurred in the West). However, if after a country had received the Faith it was later attacked by foreign invaders, its ruler would seek to defend the Faith and land. The Ethiopians' idea of defending the culture and nation that had been given them by God is very different from the Western idea of extending the Faith through the sword.

At the end of the nineteenth century, Emperor Menelik II and Empress Taytu faced a most difficult period. The nation was attacked by Italy. Up until then, Ethiopia had been free of any colonial power. Now she was being attacked by a nation with much more sophisticated military equipment. So, they gathered—bishops and priests, monks and nuns, hermits and lay people—to pray and fast and cry out to God. They brought the *tabot*, the Holy Ark into the battle. God came to their assistance. Although the other armies depended on their modern weaponry, the Ethiopians came out with spears and archers. What was known as the Battle of Aduwa turned out to be a decisive victory for Ethiopia, a humiliating lesson for Italy, and a testimony for those who struggle against oppression and put their trust in God.

## His Imperial Majesty Haile Selassie I

As long as people have lived the faith, they have had to carry the Cross. The Lord Jesus Christ said, "If anyone will come after Me, first let him deny himself, take up his cross daily and follow after Me." (Lk. 9:23) In recent times, the Cross has come to the land of Ethiopia. Faithful Ethiopian Christians have been martyred for Jesus

Christ. In the 1930's, Italy attacked once again, under the direction of the Italian dictator *Il Duce,* Benito Mussolini.

This was at the beginning of the reign of His Imperial Majesty, Haile Selassie I. During this period many faithful gave their lives and countless suffered. Holy Abuna Petros was martyred as he stood for Jesus Christ and His Church. In his autobiography, one can read about the struggles that Haile Selassie I went through. During the time he was abroad, seeking assistance from other nations, the Emperor was torn. While he desired to be on hand personally to comfort and strengthen the suffering, he knew that out of duty, he had to seek support. Ethiopia's allies in the League of Nations had signed a covenant that they would come to the aid of any member nation that was unlawfully attacked. With full confidence, Haile Selassie expected them to fulfill their word. When he stood before the assembly of the League of Nations, he reminded them of their promise. He told them that God was watching, and if they broke their promise and refused to help, He would deal with them. Soon Adolf Hitler rose to power, and the war that followed became the great scourge to those very nations that refused to honor their word. These events were the "beginning of sorrows," as Jesus put it. "Nation shall rise against nation, kingdom against kingdom" (cf. Matthew 24)—the talk was of peace, but there was no peace. Instead, there came a time of suffering.

Let us review some key events in the life of His Imperial Majesty, Haile Selassie I. Of all the kings of Africa, he is the closest to us, not only in era, but also in perspective, because of his awareness of this modern age, and because of the nature of his struggles.

*July 23, 1892:* Born during severe drought in Harar in Ethiopia to Yashimabeit and Ras Makonen, viceroy to the throne. The eight previous children had died during delivery. The child was given the name Lij *Tafari* Makonen and later received the title *Ras (Head)*, and as crown regent of Ethiopia became known as Ras Tafari.

*November 2, 1930:* As Crown Prince Ras Tafari (his name before becoming emperor) he is crowned as Emperor of Ethiopia. He was Crowned Haile Selassie I (which means the Power of the Trinity), King of Kings, King of Zion, conquering Lion of the Seed of Judah. These titles were given to the three hundred and thirty other Ethiopian emperors in succession going back to King Menelik, son of King Solomon and the Queen of Sheba (Makeda).

*June 30, 1936:* He spoke prophetically before the League of Nations in Geneva, Switzerland. His words to the League of Nations were "today

51

it is us, tomorrow it will be you." The world leaders ignored Haile Selassie's warnings and continued to recognize and support Italy's belligerence in Ethiopia. It took only three years for the Emperor's prophetic words to come to pass with the official start of World War II.

*May 5, 1941:* Exactly five years after he left Ethiopia to seek help for his country, he returned after regaining control from the invading Italians. All of Ethiopia gathered to him on that day and he said, "On this day *Ethiopia indeed stretches out her hands to God,* shouting and telling her joy to her own sons."

*September 12, 1974:* He is overthrown by the military, led by Colonel Haile Mengistu Mariam, who without any basis in reality claimed that the Emperor was too "old mentally and physically to continue any longer in office." So as not to provoke any civil war, the army worked carefully on the mind of the masses, whose reverence for His Imperial Majesty was renowned. They used the television media as a means for a well-orchestrated propaganda campaign to denigrate the Emperor.

*August 27, 1975:* Haile Selassie is martyred. He was reported to have been suffocated at the hands of lawless men. Thus, this righteous Emperor laid down his life for the defense of ancient Christianity. He, too, is a Cross-bearer.

*Fr. Paisius Altschul*

# HOLY IMAGES

Flight into Egypt.

St. Cyprian of Carthage.

St. Isaac, disciple of St. Anthony the Great, founder of monasteries
in Fayoum, south of Cairo.

The Monastery of El Baramos, where St. Moses the Black labored. His relics are preserved there.

St. Moses the Black, icon from the Monastery of El Baramos, Egypt.

SS. Apollo and Abib.

St. John the Dwarf, co-struggler with St. Paisius the Great.

St. Macarius the Great.

SS. Irene and Sofia.

# INHERITORS OF
# SUFFERING CHRISTIANITY

Nun Catherine working on the cover icon of St. Moses.
(Photo by Kim Charles Ferrill.)

Fr. Moses Berry.

William Berry, born in slavery (1848-1917).

Tombstone of William Berry, in the Resurrection Cemetery,
formerly the Berry Cemetery. William Berry,
Fr. Moses' great-grandfather, bought the land in 1872.

Caroline Boone Berry, William's wife (1850-1914).

Della Berry, William's daughter (1891-1917).

Wallace White's cabin, which served as a house-church. Built with his own hands, it is still standing.

Wallace and Daisy White, in front of their canebrake.

Wallace White (*seated at right*) with members of the Missouri 6th Cavalry, with which he served in the Civil War.

Harrison White (*at right*), son of Wallace and Daisy, with fellow soldiers during the Spanish-American War.

Three of Wallace's daughters: (*left to right*) Mamie (Fr. Moses' grandmother), Susanne and Kate.

Mamie's husband, Luther Berry (*at right*) (1893-1951).

Charles Berry, Fr. Moses' father (1925-1973) (*at left*), and Charles' brother, Fred (1929-1994), on the Berry farm, Ash Grove, Missouri.

# II
# LEGACY

# 5

# THE CHALLENGE OF MEEKNESS: AN EXERCISE IN MODERN-DAY CHRISTIAN APOLOGETICS

## NUN CATHERINE WESTON

*They that wait upon the Lord shall renew their strength;*
*they shall mount up with wings as eagles;*
*they shall run, and not be weary;*
*they shall walk, and not faint.*
—Isaiah 40:31

A NEW FORM OF APOLOGETICS is called for today because a new form of warfare is being waged against Christ's Church. Traditionally, apologetic theology has been the science of demonstrating the truth of the Christian faith through history and philosophy. It assumes that anyone who sincerely hungers for the truth can be brought to the living Truth, Jesus Christ, by a demonstration of that truth. But this is a nihilistic age, in which the fundamental, God-given belief in the existence of ultimate truth is being eroded from man's soul, to be replaced with vague contentions that all religions are complementary elements of Religion as a whole, and all monotheistic religions serve the same God. Many people do not ask themselves if Christianity is *true,* but rather if it is "right for them," and in the special case of African-Americans, if it is ethnically "compatible." As Christians, we need to be ready to answer questions at the level on which they are asked, with the hope that those who are concerned only with issues like ethnic compatibility will awaken to a hunger for truth, once the outward stumbling blocks are removed. While countless black Americans have been nurtured on Christianity from the cradle, and have found a lifetime of solace and strength in it, others, especially among the young, find the Christian value of *meekness* to be a barrier to faith. They see it as a device that the slave master used to keep their forefathers docile and in bondage. We need an adequate response to their dilemma.

There are many poetic allusions to the similarity between the sufferings of the Hebrew slaves exiled in Egypt and the sufferings of the African slaves exiled in America. Less is said about the relationship of the sufferings of the Jewish nation under the Roman yoke, to those of African-Americans under the yoke of a predominantly European culture. There are obvious differences. The blacks in America do not constitute a semi-autonomous nation, as the Jews did within the Roman Empire. Blacks do not have a separate legal structure or one unifying religion. But in both cases, the reality of oppression is felt just as keenly; the palpable longing for the fullness of liberty is felt just as strongly. The liberty thirsted for is the same: the right of a people to lead a life of dignity, to determine their own values under God, to live without the constant interference of undermining forces. Finally, in both cases anger is confused with zeal, and so yoked to aspiration as its necessary, driving force.

Think of the fifth chapter of Matthew, the "Sermon on the Mount." Jesus stands on a rolling hill overlooking the calm Sea of Galilee. It is a natural amphitheater, and his voice travels easily to the most distant listener. Freedom-hungry Jews have traveled many dusty miles to hear what the young rabbi will say. Perhaps he will be the one to lead them to victory over the Romans. Let us take the liberty of interspersing in the crowd, modern-day African-Americans, hearing Christ's words for the first time with none of the "take-it-for-grantedness" that comes from years of inattentive exposure. Will not both Jew and black listen to Christ with parallel hopes and desires? "Blessed are the poor in spirit: for theirs is the kingdom of heaven. Blessed are they that mourn: for they shall be comforted." This is a strange and unexpected doctrine, hard to grasp. Then, into the people's collective and swelling yearning comes, "Blessed are the meek." The *meek!* It comes like a knife, dividing people from each other and within their own hearts. Who, longing to throw off the yoke of oppression, whether it is the tyrannical Roman political machine, or American discrimination and injustice, wants to hear about meekness? Who takes time to ask Christ what He means before reacting, turning away, calling Him a friend of the oppressor, and not of the oppressed?

Jesus continues. "Blessed are the meek *for they shall inherit the earth.*" But an inheritance must be *waited* for. The inheritor grows and matures gradually over many years. The owner dies, and the heir receives what he is now ready for. The Prodigal Son wanted his portion *now*—and was not able to handle it. Who waits to find out that the earth which he will inherit is his own resurrected body, which can only be gained through a life lived according to the Beatitudes? St. Leo the Great says:

> This is not to be reckoned a small or cheap inheritance, as if it were distinct from our heavenly dwelling, since it is no other than [the meek and gentle] who are understood to enter the kingdom of heaven. The earth, then, which is promised to the meek, and is to be given to the gentle in possession, is the flesh of the saints, which in reward for their humility will be changed in a happy resurrection, and be clothed with the glory of immortality, in nothing now to act contrary to the spirit, and to be in complete unity and agreement with the will of the soul.[32]

A happy inheritance that, to have soul and body in perfect harmony abiding in God's will! The Prodigal received his prematurely. Instead of experiencing harmony, he was overcome by his passions and ended up eating with the swine. How does God prepare and school us for this inheritance? Often through tribulation, for ". . . we must through much tribulation enter into the kingdom of God." (Acts 14:22) Thus were the Jews, through the tribulation of slavery, prepared for the Promised Land.

## The Pattern of Meekness

But what about meekness? Is it really what the Jews thought? Or what that Ethiopian-American teenager thought when he told his mother that he was attracted to Islam because Muslims can fight back? None of this "turn the other cheek" for him. St. Nikolai Velimirovich gives a beautiful homily on meekness in his *Prologue.*[33] He expounds on Numbers 12:3—"Now the man Moses was very meek, above all the men which were upon the face of the earth." But wait—Moses was the great liberator who freed the Jewish nation from captivity and who captured the hearts and imaginations of African slaves in America! The old Negro spiritual says, "Go down Moses, way down south to Egypt land. Tell ol' Pharaoh to let my people go." The people named Harriet Tubman "Moses." Through Moses' prayers the multitude was fed on manna in the wilderness. Through Christ's prayers the multitude was fed on bread. Moses is exactly what an oppressed people want, and what the Jews wanted Christ to be. Would He be their great, strong Moses—willing and able to strike the Romans with plagues, and lead His people to freedom?[34] Yes, but not the way they expected. The Kingdom, He said, is *within*—it is an interior freedom that He offers.

Christ is meek. Moses is meek. What is this meekness? Is it really weakness? St. Nikolai says that Moses was

> . . . a type of the Lord Jesus Christ in his marvels, a victor in Egypt and in the wilderness, a leader of the people—how could he not be proud? But if he had been proud, Moses would not have been what he was. They become proud who think that they act in their own strength and not in God's. But the great Moses knew that he was a doer of God's works, and that the power with which he did them was God's power and not his. "The Lord is my strength and my song" (Ex. 15:2), said Moses.[35]

In the wilderness, Bishop Nikolai observes, Moses felt his personal weakness more than any other man—*and therefore*—prayed to God constantly for every need of the people. He prayed continually, relentlessly, never flagging or growing despondent during their journey through the wilderness. Moses was meek before God, accepting the call to be a prophet in his old age. He was meek before the people. He was not angered by their constant murmuring during the forty-year trial, because he perceived that they were really criticizing God, and not him, the mere instrument of God's will. "The Lord heareth your murmurings which ye murmur against him: and what are we? Your murmurings are not against us, but against the LORD." (Ex. 16:18)

Moses demonstrates an essential pattern for the spiritual struggle that is at the heart of every true Christian life. He trusts God absolutely; he puts no trust in his own powers at all; he prays without ceasing; he struggles without despondency.[36] Where was his self-esteem? He esteemed himself to be the handiwork and instrument of God. The chief value of a tool or instrument lies, after all, in who is using it and not in the tool itself. A fine painter can make a masterpiece with a split brush, but the finest brush in the hands of the inept is worth nothing. Time and time again, God has deliberately chosen split brushes to display His absolute virtuosity. Moses, the great prophet, was a stutterer. God gave him Aaron as a spokesman, not because He could not heal Moses, or work through him as he was, but because in his humility Moses asked for a helper. God hears the humble.

David, the prophet-king, the greatest poet of all time, the restored penitent, further illustrates the quality of humility. He testifies of himself in the Book of Psalms:

> Remember, O Lord, David and all his meekness.
> How He made an oath unto the Lord, and vowed unto the God of Jacob:
> I shall not go into the dwelling of my house, I shall not ascend upon the bed of my couch,
> I shall not give sleep to mine eyes, nor slumber to mine eyelids, nor rest to my temples,
> Until I find a place for the Lord, a habitation for the God of Jacob.
> (Ps. 131:1-5)

Blessed Augustine cites the above passage and goes on to say about the vow:

> David himself vowed as though he had it in his power, and prayed to God to fulfill his vow. There is devotion in the vow, but there is humility in the prayer. Let no one presume to think he fulfilled by his own strength what he had vowed. He, who exhorts you to vow, Himself aids you to fulfill.[37]

A bold vow that only a meek man would have the courage to make, for "God resisteth the proud, but giveth grace to the humble." (Jas. 4:6) Here the mighty king, who has the prerogative to take his ease, chooses instead to labor, to strive unceasingly, until he has found a place of rest for the Lord. What place of rest did David find? Blessed Augustine says:

> If he was meek, he sought it in himself. For how is one a place for the Lord? Hear the prophet: "Upon whom shall My Spirit rest? Even upon him that is poor and of a contrite spirit, and trembleth at my words." (cf. Isa. 66:1-2) Do you wish to be a place for the Lord? Be poor in spirit and contrite and trembling at the word of God, and you will yourself be made what you seek.[38]

If a man is poor in spirit, contrite, and trembles at the word of God, God's spirit will rest upon him. To tremble at the word of God means to fear to break even the least of His commandments. The man who keeps each of God's commandments in his heart becomes like the Ark of the Covenant. David also demonstrates the same fourfold pattern that Moses did. Remembering that he himself is meek and humble, he puts all his hope in God for the fulfillment of his vow, he desires to become a temple of the Lord, a place of continual prayer, and strives without ceasing until God hears him.

The Apostle Paul's persecutors vowed neither to eat nor drink until they had killed him (cf. Acts 23:21). These forty men made their vow in self-righteousness, out of pride and hardness of heart, and the Lord scattered their plans like dust. We don't know what their fate was. Whether they broke their vow or starved is not recorded. The meek man, thinking only of God's will, hastens to do the impossible, knowing that it will be performed by grace. In contrast, the proud man trusts in himself and the self-righteous man trusts in a god of his own devising. God resists them both and lets them fall into their own snares (cf. Ps. 34:9).

In fourth-century Africa, an Egyptian monk by the name of Paul, upwards of eighty years of age, was told by his monastic mentor, Anthony the Great, to cast the demon out of a certain suffering pilgrim. At first Paul, in deep humility, said to the demon, "Father Anthony saith, 'Go forth from this man.'" When there was no response he said, "Wilt thou go forth, or must I go and tell Christ, yea Jesus? For . . . great woe shall come upon thee." And he made an astonishing vow to the Lord—that he, an old, withered man, would stand on a rock in the blazing Egyptian sun, and not come down, or eat or drink until he died, unless God had fulfilled his prayer! What happened? The demon was cast out immediately and forcefully by the power of meekness.[39]

## Meekness in Battle

There are powerful examples in our own day that are reminiscent of the Old Testament feats of Joshua, who brought down the walls of Jericho through the power of the Ark of the Covenant (cf. Jsh. 6: 1-27), and Gideon, who defeated the Midianites with a small army hand-picked by God (cf. Jdgs. 6:11-7:25). In 1896 the Ethiopians routed the Italians in the famed Battle of Aduwa. For four months the two nations had been fighting. The Italians, under General Baratieri, also counted in their ranks conscripted Africans. The Ethiopians, numbering about 90,000, were armed with spears and some secondhand European rifles. Baratieri's army of 20,000 had been reduced to about 14,500, but they were armed with heavy artillery including sixty cannons. The Italians were outnumbered six to one but that was not unusual. Invading European armies were outnumbered throughout the African continent and were victorious—colonizing everywhere but Ethiopia. The Italians relied on their superior arms, but the Ethiopians meekly relied on God, going first to their churches and bringing out their *tabots* or arks.[40] As Aduwa is only about twenty miles from Axum, the traditional Ethiopian home of the original Hebrew Ark, many believe that the Ark itself aided in the victory. King Menelik II and his Queen, the monks and hermits and all the people came out prayerfully to the battle, and they routed the Europeans decisively through the power of meekness.[41] We can go even further and state that the Ethiopians not only prayed before battle, but actually waged war in a spirit of meek, brotherly love. They did not fight with bloodlust against the Italians, but rather, in the spirit of self-sacrifice, each vied for a spot in the front lines, so as to be first to lay his life down for his brother-soldier.[42]

In the Second World War, in 1942, the Germans were routed in the pivotal battle at El Alamein, a coastal town dedicated to the warrior saint, St. Menas [also spelled *Mina*]. Under Rommel, they had captured most of North Africa. If El Alamein had fallen, the Germans would have had a clear shot at Alexandria. They had recently defeated the Greeks, and the remainder of the Greek army had fled to Egypt, joining forces with other Allied troops. At midnight on the eve of the battle, Orthodox believers saw St. Menas in armor coming out of the ruins of his church. He was leading a caravan of camels, just as he is depicted in his icons, and heading into the ranks of the German troops. They scattered in confusion in the ensuing battle. Recognizing this to be the intervention of a saint of God, the Allies offered to return the church site to the Alexandrian Patriarchate, in order that the church might be rebuilt in St. Menas' honor. We cannot know if St. Menas responded to the prayers of the faithful Greeks and Copts in the army, or to the humble prayers that had been offered up for generations in his church for the protection of the land. If the latter is the case, it is the more profound demonstration, in that it shows the power of the simple, regular prayers of ordinary believers.[43]

In our own country, let us not forget how the Civil War, which President Lincoln fought with the primary objective of saving the Union, also freed the slaves. Was this merely a result of military expediency? After all, it provided fresh, willing recruits for the Union army and at the same time crippled the Southern economy. Or was it in a very real sense the result of generations of heartfelt prayers by the slaves themselves for freedom? Many masters forbade them to pray for fear that they would beseech God for that very thing. The slaves prayed fervently, with tears, in secret, by night—in caves, in holes dug in the fields—that the Good Lord would bring an end to their bondage. Many prayed with each stroke of the lash on their torn and bleeding backs, "Lord, have mercy!" How could God not look with compassion on such heartfelt and trusting prayers? Can we not then say that the slaves were emancipated through the power of meek supplication to the Lord?[44] Can we not also hope that the souls of countless slaves were saved through the power of meekness?

## Meekness, Action and Freedom

From the Christian perspective, meekness is not a behavior, but a virtue. All virtues are the fruits of underlying activity. We can use the analogy of an apple tree. There are years of growth and maturation before the tree is ready to bear. Then, in the spring, it puts forth leaves and flowers. Finally, the long-awaited fruit, the culmination of its growth and the reason for its existence, appears. Meekness is also a fruit, the result of many years of interior growth. It manifests as mildness—a lack of anger towards men, and a fear of God—a fear of transgressing God's commandments, and of losing His precious grace. On a more inward level, it is the state of being empty of oneself, or, more precisely, the continual act of self-emptying.[45] Perhaps on the surface it may look like being a subservient man-pleaser, but in reality it never is. Man-pleasing is a defense mechanism, a surface behavior that often has seething anger behind it. Therefore, it is hypocrisy.

True meekness, on the other hand, is the attribute of one who fully trusts in God and His providence. The person who fully trusts in God is not fighting his own battles. He doesn't take attacks against him personally. God is his advocate, his judge, his jury and his avenger. The truly meek person knows, like Moses, that if he lives his life in meek submission to God's will, those who fight against him are fighting not him, but God, and He will avenge Himself. One who fully trusts in God sees all the circumstances of his life as blessings, even if they are the blessing of a bitter medicine. Meekness is the attribute of a man who is humble in recognizing the ravages of sin in himself. It is the attribute of a man without self-pity, who, like the monk Paul, seeks God's will without caring about the personal consequences. Meekness is the attribute of a man who prays constantly in the name of Jesus, and having daily experience of the Lord fighting his spiritual battles for him, looks for victory at the hands of God, not trusting in his own prowess, and giving God the glory for his victories.

Meekness is an attribute of the man who is filled with the Holy Spirit:

> . . . for on this account the Holy Spirit has been manifested to us in a dove and in fire; because, to wit, all whom He fills He causes to shew themselves as meek with the simplicity of the dove, and burning with

the fire of zeal. He then is in nowise full of the Holy Spirit, who either in the calm of meekness forsakes the fervor of zeal, or again, in the ardor of zeal loses the virtue of meekness.[46]

Here, from St. Gregory the Great, we have the solution to the riddle of the meekness of Moses, of David, of Joshua, of Gideon—indeed of all the powerful figures of the Old and New Testaments. They were all chosen vessels of the Holy Spirit and so combined in themselves, through His grace, meekness and zeal. We remember them for their zeal, but that zeal was empowered by meekness.

Meekness is at home in Africa in a strong and powerful way. At home in Moses; in the great monks Anthony and Paul, and in a countless multitude of the disciples of these monastic fathers. Meekness is at home in the victors of the battles of Aduwa and El Alamein. It is not something that African-Americans need to be ashamed or afraid of in Christianity. Although the oppressor may have waved something in the face of African slaves and their descendants that was labeled "the Christian duty of meekness," *true* meekness is not a value of the oppressor—it is his worst enemy. It was Pharaoh's worst enemy because the vengeance was the Lord's (cf. Rom 12:19). It was the worst enemy of St. Paul's persecutors, because they fraudulently imitated the boldness of the meek. It was the worst enemy of the Italians at Aduwa, because through meek prayer, spears overcame rifles. Meekness is all-powerful, but it comes at a price, that of living according to the fourfold precepts that Moses and David demonstrated—not relying on oneself in anything, all-daring trust in God alone, unceasing prayer, and untiring striving for good.

God wills, always and for all people, freedom from the passions of anger, hate, jealousy, bitterness—the very ones that are so often aroused by oppression. These passions are themselves oppressors, striking the weak as well as the mighty. It is also God's will that we give thanks, in whatever situation we find ourselves (cf. I Thes. 5:18), trusting in His providence for good, trusting that He will hear our prayers. His will may well be for political freedom, as when He sent Moses to the enslaved Hebrews. But remember, they had to wait on God's time, four hundred years, before they were mature enough in His eyes to inherit the Promised Land.

Some of the chief freedoms African-Americans long for today are not exclusively political. Receiving the vote did not change everything. Freedom from poor education, from drug dealers, from urban violence; freedom to earn an honest and adequate living; freedom to live in a nonviolent neighborhood, in suitable, affordable housing. Surely these desires must be in accordance with God's will! Can the evils of our day succumb to the power of meekness? Christ said, "Woe unto the world because of offenses! for it must needs be that offenses come . . ." (Mt. 18:7) and, "ye have the poor always with you." (Mt. 26:11) But hear the Lord's comforting promise:

> If my people, which are called by my name, shall humble themselves, and pray, and seek my face, and turn from their wicked ways; then will I hear them from heaven, and will forgive their sin, and will heal their land. (II Chron. 7:4)

Who, then, has prepared himself morally, who has the courage to stand on the high rock with Paul the monk and say, "Lord, I will not come down from the height of my prayer until You cast the demons of sin, of ignorance, of vice out of me, out of my suffering neighbor, my suffering neighborhood, my suffering land!"

*This talk, presented at the Third Annual Ancient Christianity and African-American Conference, was inspired by the writings of St. Nikolai Velimirovich, who spoke in 1921 to a group of 1,500 African-Americans at St. Philips Episcopal Church in Harlem, the church Mother Catherine grew up in.*

# 6

# LOST HERITAGE
# OF
# AFRICAN-AMERICANS

FR. MOSES BERRY

WRITING THIS ARTICLE has been one of the most difficult tasks I've ever undertaken. Many, many years ago, my grandmother, Dorothy, told me to be careful about how much information I shared with the world outside our family. She said, "If you
share something sacred with people who won't respect it, they will
try to reduce it to something that they can understand, and miss the
sacredness." "Therefore," she said, "don't let them know about your
church music because they'll turn it into dance music or look at it
like 'folk music,' and miss the point that it's the music of suffering
people that lifted them from earth to heaven. It's not merely an art
form." I have carefully guarded what was handed down to me by my
forefathers and mothers, but now we're in such difficult days, that if
only one person can be touched by what I've been given, I'll take
the risk of having our pearls trampled underfoot.

The African-American community today faces very difficult times.
This is especially true concerning its young people. Daily their reality is shaped by the negative image of them portrayed in the media,
which becomes a sort of self-fulfilling prophecy. They seem like
they're floundering and aimless. Some of the strongest youth leaders today—the "gangsta rappers," for instance—bring negative influences that seem to creep in and steer our children towards lawlessness.

I believe that this is a time in which false Christs are rising up. Jesus Christ Himself told us, "If they say, 'Lo, he is in the desert,' don't believe it. If they say He is in another place don't believe it." There is a certain sort of counterfeit Christianity that is abounding these days, and it sounds almost like the real thing. It says things like, "We need to return to family values." Most have heard this statement. It is essentially correct. We do need to return to teaching our children proper values. But the real problem is deeper and wider than that, and it has its source in the fallen nature of man.

We must prepare ourselves, because even more difficult days lie ahead. I believe we are seeing what Scripture calls the "last days," or end times. We, as African-American people, are in store for a time that has never come before, and will never come again.

The Lord has told us that in end times, "if it weren't for the sake of the elect, no flesh would be saved." Knowing this, and that we are a minority and the low man on the social totem pole in America, we can expect that if times become more difficult for everyone, they will be especially difficult for us.

## That Old Time Religion

Many Americans say that we need to return to a time when God was present in our culture and He was honored everywhere. The fallacy of this kind of thinking is that it assumes that there was such a time. It makes it seem as if there was a generation that didn't experience the effects of the Fall and in which man didn't suffer, and we know that's not the case. There is a cemetery on my family's property that is over one hundred years old. The oldest gravestone we found there was from 1863. In that era (that "good time" that so many people wish to return to), black people were not allowed to be buried in white cemeteries. Sometimes they were left along the side of the road. They weren't buried in consecrated graveyards. As a result, my great-grandparents, having homesteaded in the Ozarks after the Civil War, took part of their property and set it aside for a graveyard for African-American people, and Native Americans.

As long as I can remember, I have been proud of being named after my great-grandfather, Wallace White, who was the first and only black man in Company D, 6th Missouri Union Calvary. He was also the only member of Company D not to receive a military pension. In spite of this great injustice, he was thankful for what he had, and taught his children and grandchildren never to be resentful and always to "bless those that curse you."

It was through this righteous elder "Uncle Wallace's" daughter

Mamie, my grandmother, that I was taught otherworldly Christian values. My grandmother used to tell us that what matters is not whether you are rich or poor, but how you prepare yourself for the life to come. She would say that we must prepare ourselves in life by hard work and education, but that these efforts were only things to do until we met the Lord—not ends in and of themselves. The most important thing in life was to break away from the hold that this present world has on people, making us forget what we are made for, which is to love God before all else, and our neighbor as ourself. I was born only 86 years after the end of slavery, in the twilight of a near-forgotten era, when this country was dotted with survivors of slavery and their children. Former slaves were alive in my child-hood. Mamie's father was a slave. These people knew, because of their experience here, that this world was not their true home, and they lived in the hope of the Kingdom of Heaven, or as they put it, "always looking beyond the blue."

My other grandmother, Dorothy, used to say to me, "Remember, son, I don't call you 'son' because you're mine, I call you 'son' be-cause you shine. Jesus said, 'My kingdom is not of this world. If it were, my disciples would fight for it.' Don't get all wrapped up in the cares and worries of this world. Don't forget that you are a mi-nority in America, and this is not your world." This was the world-view of the generation that raised me.

## How We Lost What We Had—
## or, "You Can't Spend What You Ain't Got"

African-Americans have never been equals in this country, and any peace which we have enjoyed has come from God Almighty. We didn't come here willingly, but were brought as captives, so if we ever expect to find a home here, we cannot look for it "in the world." Our forefathers knew this, and they looked for that home beyond this vale of tears, in that "old time religion." Even those who weren't particularly spiritually minded knew that they should be, and most of them had at least part of the Gospel of Jesus Christ taught to them. If they rejected the Gospel, it was out of choice, not ignorance. Perhaps this is why they were, as the Gospel says, "beaten with many stripes."

Our present crisis, which is a spiritual one, had its beginnings in social integration. I won't say that integration was the downfall of the black man in this country, but it did present a real problem. When we were segregated, it was very clear that we were not "of this world." I'm not suggesting that it was ever a heavenly existence for us, but we did not look for our peace here and now, but in the world to come.

When blacks started thinking that we could be anything in this country that we wanted to be, the confusion began because, in fact, we couldn't. We began to live under the illusion that we could find happiness in the land of opportunity, when in reality we were second-class citizens. We were even told that there was a remedy for racism—that malady planted in the hearts of men by the evil one. Racism can no more be legislated away than greed and lust. We lost the world-view of our elders, and forgot "our place." While it is true that some African-Americans were able to enjoy the lifestyle of the majority, for the masses it was only the promise of a dream that was conceived, but never achieved. Of course, it is also true that other races and nationalities have been unable to find peace pursuing worldly success. However, there is only one race in this country that has had to have legislation passed repeatedly in order for its children to attend school with others, or eat a hot dog at the same lunch counter. We, of all peoples, should have remembered that this world was not for us, regardless of what the well-meaning "progressives" told us.

Now, more than forty years since *Brown v. Board of Education* mandated integration of the public schools, we find ourselves in a situation that is the direct result of wanting what is not ours to have. Black school children in the late '50's and early '60's began to spout rhetoric given them from white teachers. "You are just as good as anyone else." Of course we were! We knew we were just as smart as the white children and in fact resented the implication that we might not be. Our elders had taught us that God loved us as He loved "all the flowers in His garden," as my mother used to say. What was new was the suggestion that we *could be anything we wanted to be*. It was a lie, and we began to lose our bearings. We took our eye off the genuine prize, which is otherworldly Christianity, and we started focusing on what we could attain in this present world. We have bought into every idea that the national advertising industry waves in front of us. We have succumbed to the desire to make everything in this world belong to us whether it was for us to have or not. They told our women that blondes have more fun, and lo and behold, the black woman dyed her hair. How absurd!

Nowadays we have forgotten how to be poor—how to make the best of what little you have without resenting not having everything that's put out in the marketplace. How to be thankful to God for everything He brings our way. There are stories of slaves who were beaten until their bones were bare, and at each fall of the lash on their backs would cry "Lord, have mercy." Even in their extremity they remembered God. We have forgotten Him in our abundance, crying only, "I want more." Some "at-risk" African-American youths have to have everything their passions dictate, but they were never given the knowledge of right livelihood. Many are generations-removed from making their living by the "sweat of their brow." Only with faith in God is it possible to endure hardship with grace and integrity. There are countless cases of boys and girls growing up without any idea of what they are alive for. They haven't been taught that God loves them no matter what situation they find themselves in, and they haven't been prepared to get along in a world which never has, and never will, love them. All they know is that they have to take what they want. They live under the illusion of their "entitlement" to that which they desire. They have succumbed to the most extreme manifestation of the nihilism that characterizes our age.

## Who We Are

In order to reach out to our people, we need a sense of our own cultural heritage. It's kind of confusing, however, because recently we have been taught that we are not black. We've been taught that we are just people, like anyone else. We are simply Americans, "just folks." On a certain level that's true. But you would never hear the Russians, for example, say, "We're just folks." They're proud of being Russian. You never hear the Greeks say, "We're just folks." They put it right on their church: "Greek Orthodox!" There is a reason for this: it brings their people along as a whole. It keeps their eyes focussed on the fact that they as a community are moving together.

Likewise, we can't be ashamed of our African heritage. Some people have asked me why we can't do away with the "African" in African-American. After all, we're all Americans, right? My answer is that there are many groups within this nation, and they are simply not all the same. Of course, in Christ there is no East or West, nor bond nor free, nor Jew nor Gentile. But among men, this is not the case. I have heard my well-meaning, so-called "conservative" brothers say that they don't consider themselves "African-Americans." Furthermore, some say, "I'm not just African, I'm multi-racial as a result of slavery or intermarriage." Nevertheless we are an African-American people. However much we may be mixed up with other folks, we will always be identified, if not by ourselves, then by others, as black.

This point was made very clear in a story told about Vernon

Johns, a famous African-American preacher, and a hero of mine. The ordinary people in his church were very proud of him. One of his deacons was just bursting with pride, and said, "Oh, Pastor, it is so wonderful that you have accomplished these great deeds, and now, you're a Ph.D.!" And Vernon Johns, in his typical manner, turned to his deacon and said, "Deacon, do you know what they call a Negro with a Ph.D.?" The deacon tried to figure it out, and said, "Well. . . . It doesn't come to me." Vernon replied, "You know what they call him? They call him a nigger. Just like everybody else." So, whether we want to believe it or not, we are all in the same boat. And we do live in the world. We owe it to ourselves, to our children, to the generations that follow us to—not to be proud of our African-American heritage in and of itself, but to take pride in it as something that was made by God. God doesn't err, and He wants all of His people to be exalted, not only exalted together, but also exalted individually. We are each made in His image and after His likeness. I always remember the words of Phillis Wheatley, the great poet, "Even darkies as black as cane may become refined, and join the angelic train."[47] [Wheatley was a slavewoman in colonial times, who wrote God-inspired poetry—poetry so fine that the educated critics refused to believe it could come from such a humble source.]

## To the Praying Ground

As Christians, we cannot be so shallow as to blame the disasters in the black community on a liberal political agenda. This is the wisdom of the world which we know is folly to God. I am shaken when Christians of good will point their fingers at politics as the source of our troubles. The truth is that we war against powers and principalities that have set themselves against us since we set foot on these shores. In our sufferings, we were made strong by the hand of the Almighty, and this confounded Satan and his minions, who have now ravaged our youth. Only one thing can save them, and that is to return to that otherworldly Christianity that is their rightful inheritance from the blood and prayer of their ancestors.

Brigid Wingo was someone in my own life who tried to show me the way. She didn't want me to perish. When I was young, I was quite wild and lawless. Later on, I gave my first sermon at the Donovan Chapel A.M.E. Church. Mrs. Wingo, an elderly lady, got up in the middle of the congregation and gave a testimony about me. She said, "All the time you were doing all those naughty and bad things I was praying that the Lord would do something with you. I'm responsible for this!" In retrospect, it was a funny thing for her to say, but that day no one laughed. We looked at her and knew she was right. She was not willing to see me perish.

This once-shunned piety is exactly what we need in these desperate times to help us and our young people climb out of the nihilistic pit dug for us by the pernicious serpent—who seeks to drag us down to hell alive, while at the same time destroying the rich legacy left us by previous generations of suffering Christian elders.

Christians have been anointed to preach the Gospel to everyone and not to withhold from anyone. Many of us are guilty of withholding the Gospel from our young people. You've perhaps heard the expression "lost generation" used to describe them. We can't write them off and then wonder why they are in the condition that they are in. I believe that this generation of African-American youth is profoundly sensitive and truth-seeking. They have succumbed to lawlessness and nihilism because they see through the façade of this world, and yet no one shows them the way out. Perhaps we say to ourselves, "But I pray for them." But do we hear what the Lord says to us? "Go into all the world and preach Him." Often we do not hear or we make excuses. Yet this is the very thing we must do in order to save our young people. Believe me, all of our people are perishing, not only the young. The so-called "stable families" are perishing. We, as Christian men and women, are not reaching out to them in such a way as to bring them to the knowledge of Christ.

We despise the downtrodden among us and we judge them. We say, secretly, that they are not of our caliber. But we don't know a thing about these people. We don't know how many nights they have watered their couch with tears saying, "O Lord, send someone to save me. Help me, for I am perishing." Although we often see them perishing, we don't reach out to give them "one cool drink of water." We are guilty of this, and if the situation doesn't change we are all going to perish together.

**Seeds**

One day, I awoke spiritually, as a result of those seeds that were planted by my elders long ago. I came to my senses like the Prodigal Son did. First, he left a good home. Then after much suffering, he came to his senses. But if he had never had that good seed planted in him, he would have awakened to nothingness, to confusion, not knowing where to go or what to do. When the Prodigal awoke he said, "In my father's house the servants live better than I do. I know what I'll do, I'll go to my father and ask for forgiveness." He had the memory of goodness sown deep within him. We need to plant good

71

seed in our brothers and sisters, and not be ashamed to go and reach out to them. God forbid that we say within ourselves, "They will never receive it. They are too dense."

To illustrate this I want to relate a story about Abbot Herman Podmoshensky, my spiritual father. Once he came to Atlanta when I lived there. He saw a brochure for the "Pan-African orthodox church." This church was known to be very militantly Afro-centric and African nationalist, and it often held to teachings outside of mainstream Christianity. Much to my dismay, Fr. Herman said, "Oh, we've got to go over there, Father Moses. Grab your wife and everybody. We're going to go over there." The church was located in what was considered by many to be a rough neighborhood. Fr. Herman enthusiastically said, "We're going to meet those Christians—they want to be genuine Christians." I said to him, privately, "Father Herman, they're not what some would call Christian." But he kept telling me, "Just be quiet, be quiet, we're going. We're going there to those people because they want Jesus Christ." But I protested, "They don't want Jesus Christ. Not only that, but they won't like you, because you are white, they won't like you. I know some people in the organization." And he responded, in an endearing manner, "We're going anyway." When we arrived, the building was closed for the day—there was a huge lock on the doors. We could tell, however, that there were still people inside. Fr. Herman started pounding on the doors, and I said to myself, "Oh, no, we're doomed." He had a younger monk with him, with long hair, and I thought, as I considered this skinny white boy, "Oh no, they're going to kill us." Fr. Herman continued pounding on the door, and finally someone came and asked what we wanted. He replied, "I came all the way from California to see you, I want to tell you about the Lord." They opened the door, and invited us in! Fr. Herman knew that what he had—otherworldly Orthodox Christianity—was precious. He was willing to go to extraordinary lengths to bring the Good News, even to the "Pan-African orthodox church." My uncle used to say, "If you don't think you're in the best church in the world, you must be in the wrong church."

Inside that particular church, the walls were decorated with photographs of tribal Africans. Father Herman said, "These are wonderful, but you don't have anything up there of Saint Moses!" They said, "We don't know about Saint Moses. Who's Saint Moses?" No one had told them. I myself, Father Moses, who had lived in that city so long, hadn't told them. Fr. Herman turned to me and said, "Father Moses, tell them about him." So I did, and they immediately wanted icon prints of him. We gave them one for their store, and they thanked Fr. Herman.

As we were leaving, Fr. Herman remembered that he wanted a picture from their church. They had a portrait of the Virgin as black, and he wanted one of those to take home with him. So, he had to beat on yet another door, this time, outside of their chapel. He called loudly, "Come, I want one of those pictures." A very big man appeared at the door, wearing a sleeveless T-shirt (which revealed his huge arms) with African nationalist symbols on it. He asked us what we wanted, and again, Fr. Herman said, "I want one of those pictures!" The man, to my total surprise, was moved, and said regretfully, "We don't have any, we're all out." Then he went and brought back the director of the program, who gave Fr. Herman the only print in the whole building. This happened to be her personal, prized possession, given to her and signed by their founder. Now we might think that's nothing, but it was something very dear to her. It had meaning for her and she gave it to Fr. Herman. She did this because he reached out to all of them, and didn't judge them.

The point of this story is not to tell you about my spiritual father, but to let you know that we ourselves have to be bold and reach out to our brothers and sisters, and not judge them by their outward appearance, or they will be lost. I had forgotten that many African-Americans were seeking authentic African Christianity, and no one was pointing them in the right direction.

We have to reach out to our brothers and sisters and plant seeds within them, so that when they come to their senses, they might have some idea of what to do. When they come to their senses, they will be able to find strength and blessing. In the Name of Jesus Christ, Amen.

# 7

# THE LEGACY
# OF A SUFFERING
# CHURCH:
# THE HOLINESS
# OF AMERICAN SLAVES

## PROFESSOR ALBERT RABOTEAU

*"By some amazing but vastly creative spiritual insight the slave
undertook the redemption of a religion that the master had profaned
in his midst."*
—Howard Thurman

THE HOLINESS OF AFRICAN-AMERICAN SLAVES, as the
black minister, poet, and mystic, Howard Thurman, attests, con-
sisted in their living witness—despite severe persecution and suffering—to the Christian gospel, whose truth they perceived and maintained in contradiction to the debasement of that very gospel by
those who held power over their bodies and their external actions,
but not their souls. The suffering witness of slave Christians constitutes a major spiritual legacy not only for their descendants but for
the nation as a whole, for any who would take the time to heed the
testimony of their words and of their lives.

### A Persecuted Faith

If asked to discuss the history of the persecution of Christianity,
most of us would first recall the early centuries of the Church as *the*
era of persecution, when thousands of Christians became confessors
or martyrs by suffering or dying for their faith at the hands of the

Roman authorities, until the emperor Constantine gave official state approval to Christianity in the fourth century. And we probably would mention the modern waves of persecution that swept over Christians in the twentieth century under the anti-religious regimes of Communist states in Eastern Europe. Few, I think, would identify the suffering of African-American slave Christians in similar terms, as a prime example of the persecution of Christianity within our own nation's history. And yet the extent to which the Christianity of American slaves was hindered, proscribed, and persecuted justifies applying the title "confessor" and "martyr" to those slaves who, like their ancient Christian predecessors, bore witness to the Christian gospel despite the threat of punishment and even death at the hands of fellow Christians.

The Christianity of American slaves was born in suffering, the suffering of capture, middle passage, and enslavement for life—all justified by Christian European and American defenders of slavery as a means of bringing pagan Africans to the knowledge of Christianity. For despite the physical suffering of slavery, Africans, according to this argument, would gain the spiritual benefits of Christianity and European civilization. The hypocrisy of this argument became clear when slaveholders in the Americas proved apathetic, if not downright hostile to the religious instruction of their slaves. It was the labor of Africans' bodies, not the salvation of their souls, that preoccupied the majority of slaveholders, especially in British North America, where whites feared that baptism would disrupt their system of slave control. Peter Kalm, a Swedish traveler in America from 1748-1750, outlined their antipathy to Christian slaves:

> It is . . . greatly to be pitied, that the masters of these Negroes in most of the English colonies take little care of their spiritual welfare, and let them live on in their Pagan darkness. There are even some, who would be very ill pleased at, and would by all means hinder their Negroes from being instructed in the doctrines of Christianity; to this they are partly led by the conceit of its being shameful, to have a spiritual brother or sister among so despicable a people; partly by thinking that they should not be able to keep their Negroes so meanly afterwards; and partly through fear of the Negroes growing too proud, on seeing themselves upon a level with their masters in religious matters.[48]

It is clear that Anglo-Americans feared the precise ethos that the slaves quickly recognized and valued in Christianity: the incorporation of Africans into the church community changed the relationship of master and slave into one of brother and sister in Christ, a relationship that inevitably contradicted the racist belief in black inferiority upon which slavery depended.

At first the masters reasoned that it would be illegal to hold a fellow Christian in bondage, so baptizing slaves would in effect free them. Colonial legislatures quickly passed laws stating that baptism had no such effect. Nonetheless slaveowners still resisted missions to convert the slaves. To baptize Africans seemed inappropriate since it made them more like the English, thus blurring the religious difference between blacks and whites which along with nationality, skin color, and language formed the ethnic identity of Anglo-Americans and their sense of racial superiority upon which slavery depended. Moreover, they believed that Christianity would inflate the slaves' sense of self worth and so encourage them to insolent or even rebellious behavior. Christianity, according to this view, ruined slaves. Colonial missionaries argued to the contrary that religious instruction would make slaves better slaves by stressing that Christianity made no alteration in social conditions, but taught each person to remain content in his station in life. Christianity would induce the slaves to obey their masters out of a sense of duty to God rather than merely out of fear of man. They appealed repeatedly to Ephesians 6:5: "Slaves, be obedient to your masters." Thus Christian missionaries came to propagate the gospel as a means of slave control.

Slaves eventually did hear the message of the gospel and insisted, contrary to missionaries and masters, that becoming Christian should result in their (or at least their children's) freedom. Time and again European-American clergymen complained that slaves were seeking baptism because they thought the sacrament would make them free. What the slaves affirmed and the slaveholders rejected was the belief that slavery and Christianity were incompatible—that a slaveholding Christianity was a contradiction in terms, in other words—a heresy. In one of the earliest documents we have from American slaves, they boldly confessed their belief that slavery violated the fundamental law of Christian community, the law of love:

> There is a great number of us sencear . . . members of the Church Christ. . . . Bear ye one 'nothers bordens. How can the master be said to Beare my Borden when he Beares me down with the Have chains of slavery and operson against my will. How can the slave perform the duties of a husband to a wife or parent to his child. . . [?][49]

Slaveowners were well aware that slaves interpreted Christianity as sanctioning their desire for freedom in this life as well as the next. The slaves, therefore, if they wanted to express their faith openly, had to steal away to clandestine prayer meetings in their cabins, woods, thickets, hollows, and brush arbors, the aptly named "hush harbors," nineteenth-century equivalents of the ancient catacombs. There, out from under the eye of the master, they challenged the heresy of the master's preachers with the orthodox doctrine of their own preaching. Former slave Lucretia Alexander contrasted the white preacher's version of the gospel with that of her father:

> The preacher came and he'd just say, "Serve your masters. Don't steal your master's turkey. Don't steal your master's chickens. Don't steal your master's hawgs. Don't steal your master's meat. Do whatsomever your master tells you to do." Same old thing all the time. My father would have church in dwelling houses and they had to whisper. . . . Sometimes they would have church at his house. That would be when they would want a real meetin' with some real preachin'. . . . They used to sing their songs in a whisper and pray in a whisper.[50]

As Henry Atkinson, an escaped slave from Virginia, put it, "The white clergymen don't preach the whole gospel there."[51] The hunger for "Real preachin'," that is, the authentic gospel, drove the slaves to gather their own worship services.

Slave Christians suffered severe punishment if they were caught attending secret prayer meetings which whites proscribed as a threat to social order. Moses Grandy reported that his brother-in-law Isaac, a slave preacher, "was flogged, and his back pickled" for preaching at a clandestine service in the woods. His listeners were also flogged and "forced to tell who else was there." Grandy claimed that slaves were often flogged "if they are found singing or praying at home." Gus Clark reported: "My Boss didn' 'low us to go to church, er to pray er sing. Iffen he ketched us singin' he whupped us." According to another ex-slave, "the white folks would come in when the colored people would have prayer meeting, and whip every one of them. Most of them thought that when colored people were praying it was against them. For they would catch them praying for God to lift things out of their way. . . ." Henry Bibb's master threatened him with five hundred lashes for attending a prayer meeting conducted by slaves on a neighboring plantation, without permission. The master who threatened Bibb was a deacon in the local Baptist Church.[52]

In 1792, Andrew Bryan and his brother Sampson were arrested and hauled before the city magistrates of Savannah, Georgia for holding worship services. Together with about fifty of their followers they were imprisoned twice and were severely whipped. Andrew told his persecutors "that he rejoiced not only to be whipped, but *would freely suffer death for the cause of Jesus Christ.*"[53] When the master's will conflicted with God's, slaves faced a choice, to obey God or to obey man. Many, empowered by the belief that salvation lay in obeying God rather than man, chose to disobey their masters. Eli Johnson, for example, claimed that when he was threatened with five hundred lashes for holding prayer meetings, he stood up to his master and declared, "In the name of God, why is it, that I can't after working hard all the week, have a meeting on Saturday evening? I'll suffer the flesh to be dragged off my bones . . . for the sake of my blessed Redeemer."[54] Fugitive slave James Smith had been a preacher in Virginia. To prevent him from preaching, his master kept him tied up all day on Sundays and, when he refused to stop, flogged him as well. Nevertheless, Smith kept up his ministry and later reported that "many were led to embrace the Savior under his preaching."[55]

The husband of Candace Richardson, from Mississippi, stole off to the woods to pray, "but he prayed so loud that anybody close around could hear; and so was discovered and punished." Many years later, Mrs. Richardson told interviewers that "beatings didn't stop my husband from praying. He just kept on praying and it was his prayers, and [those of] a whole lot of other slaves that cause you young folks to be free today."[56] A former slave revealed the source of their resolve:

> When I was a slave my master would sometimes whip me *awful*, specially when he knew I was praying. He was determined to whip the Spirit out of me, but he could never do it, for de more he whip the more the Spirit make me *content* to be whipt.[57]

Finally, Charlotte Martin, a former slave from Florida, told an interviewer that "her oldest brother was whipped to death for taking part in one of the religious ceremonies."[58] Unfortunately, we don't know his name, but Charlotte Martin's brother, and other slaves— unnamed and unknown—joined the company of all those Christians over the ages who have suffered brutal violence and even death to worship God in spirit and in truth. These secret liturgies constituted the heart and source of slave spiritual life, the sacred time when they brought their sufferings to God and experienced the amazing transformation of their sadness into joy.

## A Sad Joyfulness

Recalling the character of their secret religious gatherings, one former slave declared,

Meetings back there meant more than they do now. Then everbody's heart was in tune, and when they called on God they made heaven ring. It was more than just Sunday meeting and then no godliness for a week. They would steal off to the fields and in the thickets and there . . . they called on God out of heavy hearts.[59]

Exhausted from a day of work that stretched from dawn ("day clean") to after sundown, the slaves found relief and refreshment in prayer, as Richard Caruthers remembered:

Us niggers used to have a prayin' ground down in the hollow and sometime we come out of the field . . . scorchin' and burnin' up with nothin' to eat, and we wants to ask the good Lawd to have mercy. . . . We takes a pine torch . . . and goes down in the hollow to pray. Some gits so joyous they starts to holler loud and we has to stop up they mouth. I see niggers git so full of the Lawd and so happy they draps unconscious.[60]

This paradoxical combination of suffering and joy permeated slave religion, as the slave spirituals attest:

Nobody knows de trouble I see
Nobody knows but Jesus,
Nobody knows de trouble I've had
Glory hallelu![61]

The tone of joyful sadness that echoed and re-echoed in the slaves' religious worship was eloquently explained by a former slave who was initially puzzled by it himself:

The old meeting house caught on fire. The spirit was there. Every heart was beating in unison as we turned our minds to God to tell him of our sorrows here below. God saw our need and came to us. I used to wonder what made people shout, but now I don't. There is a joy on the inside, and it wells up so strong that we can't keep still. It is fire in the bones. Any time that fire touches a man, he will jump.[62]

Joyful sorrow, sorrowful joy, or more accurately, sorrow merging into joy arose from the suffering of the slaves' lives, a suffering that was touched, however, and so transformed, by the living presence of God.

We all know something of the brutality that slaves endured; and it still is painful to think of it. Yet, the mystery of their suffering took on meaning in the light of the suffering of Jesus, who became present to them in their suffering as the model and author of their faith. As one former slave explained to a missionary during the Civil War:

79

I could not hab libbed had not been for de Lord . . . neber! Work so late, and so early; work so hard, when side ache so. Chil'en sold; old man gone. All visitors, and company in big house; all cooking and washing all on me, and neber done enough. Missus neber satisfied— no hope. Noting, noting but Jesus, I look up. O Lord! how long? Give me patience! patience! O Lord! Only Jesus know how bad I feel; darsn't tell any body, else get flogged. Darsn't call upon de Lord; darsn't tell when sick. But . . . I said, "Jesus, if it your will, I will bear it."[63]

The passion of Jesus, the Suffering Servant, spoke deeply to the slaves, the sorrow and pain of their life resonating with His. For if Jesus came as the Suffering Servant, the slave certainly resembled Him more than the master. They knew that their lives fit the gospel pattern: "Blessed are the poor, for theirs is the Kingdom of Heaven. Blessed are the meek, for they shall inherit the earth. Blessed are those who hunger and thirst after righteousness, for they shall be filled."

The slaves perceived in their own experience the paradox of the gospel, the redemptive power of Christ's suffering, repeated once again in the pattern of their own lives. They believed that according to this gospel the victory of evil over good is only apparent. They believed that for those who follow His way of the cross, sadness yields to joy, despair to hope, and death to life. This was no easy faith for slaves exposed to constant toil and regular violence at the hands of professed fellow Christians. We should not underestimate the difficulty of living such beliefs. The temptations to despair, to reject Christianity as a religion for whites, to abandon belief in a God who permits the innocent to suffer were very real. Frederick Douglass, for example, spoke of "the doubts arising . . . partly from the sham religion which everywhere prevailed" under slavery, doubts which "awakened in my mind a distrust of all religion and the conviction that prayers were unavailing and delusive."[64] A free black woman named Nellie, from Savannah, Georgia, confessed

It has been a terrible mystery, to know why the good Lord should so long afflict my people, and keep them in bondage,—to be abused, and trampled down, without any rights of their own,—with no ray of light in the future. Some of my folks said there wasn't any God, for if there was He wouldn't let white folks do as they have done for so many years. . . .[65]

## Exodus

One of the sources that sustained Christian slaves against such temptations to despair was the Bible with its accounts of the mighty deeds of a God who miraculously intervenes in human history to cast down the mighty and to lift up the lowly, a God who saves the oppressed and punishes the oppressor. The biblical stories became their story. Why trust that God would deliver them? Because he had, as the spirituals recounted, fit Joshua for the battle of Jericho, rescued Daniel from the lion's den, saved the three Hebrew children from the fiery furnace, kept doubting Peter from sinking beneath the waves, comforted weeping Mary in the garden, and freed Paul and Silas from jail. "Didn't my Lord deliver Daniel? Why not every man?"

One biblical story in particular fired the imagination of the slaves and anchored their hope of deliverance: Exodus. Questioned by her mistress about her faith, a slave woman named Polly explained why she resisted despair:

> We poor creatures have need to believe in God, for if God Almighty will not be good to us some day, why were we born? When I heard of his delivering his people from bondage I know it means the poor African.[66]

The story of Exodus inculcated in the slaves (and in their descendants) a sense of being a specially chosen people, whose election and destiny were of historic importance in the providence of God. For black Americans the Exodus story took on the force of a prophecy that directly contradicted the dominant image of America as the Promised Land. From the earliest period of their migration to America, British colonists had spoken of their journey across the Atlantic as the exodus of a New Israel from bondage in Egypt to the Promised Land of milk and honey. For African-Americans the journey was reversed: whites might claim that America was a new Israel, but blacks knew that it was Egypt, since they, like the children of Israel of old, still toiled in bondage. Unless America freed God's African children, this nation would suffer the plagues that had afflicted Egypt.

Exodus proved that slavery contradicted God's will and so would inevitably end. The where and the how remained hidden in divine providence, but the promise of deliverance was certain. The racist belief that black people were destined by providence and by nature to be nothing more than drawers of water and hewers of wood was false. They were elect of God.

The slaves' sense of identification with the children of Israel was driven deep into their hearts by the song, sermon, prayer, and dance of worship. They dramatically re-enacted the travails and triumphs of God's chosen people and so affirmed and reaffirmed—contrary to racist doctrines of black inferiority—their own value as a special, divinely-chosen people. In their prayer services, biblical past became present in sacred, liturgical time and the stories they sang about came alive. Once again God sent Moses to tell "ol' Pharaoh to let my people go." Once again the mighty wind of God parted the Red Sea so the Hebrew children could cross over dry shod. Once again Pharaoh's army "got drownded."

Long after slavery, African-Americans continued to appropriate the story of Exodus to symbolize their common history and common destiny, as a specially chosen, divinely-favored people, another darker Israel denying the dominant myth of America's identity and purpose. In the midst of dehumanizing conditions so bleak that despair seemed the only appropriate response, African-Americans believed that God would "make a way out of no way." Enslaved, they predicted that God would free them from bondage. Impoverished, they asserted that "God would provide." Their belief in God did not consist so much in a set of propositions, as it did in a relationship of personal trust that God was with them:

> He have been wid us, Jesus,
> He still wid us, Jesus,
> He will be wid us, Jesus
> Be wid us to the end. (Slave Spiritual)

As some critics of black religion have long observed, an overemphasis upon religious trust can foster in oppressed people a passive and compensatory otherworldliness vulnerable to fatalism and lethargy. But religious faith also encouraged confidence among African-Americans that change was possible in this world, not just in the next, and so enabled black people to hope, and, when possible, to act. When acts of external resistance proved impossible, or suicidal, African-American spirituality supported internal resistance that was symbolic but nonetheless real. The most effective ground for resisting the demons of dehumanization and internalized racism was the slaves' firm conviction that the human person is made in the image of God.

82

## The Altar of the Heart

Drawing upon the worship traditions of Africa, as well as those of evangelical Christianity, African-American slaves formed a ritual equivalent to the spirit-empowered ceremonies of their African fore-bears. Both traditions assumed that authentic worship required an observable experience of the divine presence. "It ain't enough to talk about God, you've got to feel him moving on the altar of your heart," as one former slave explained.[67] Ritual, in this perspective, was supposed to bring the divine tangibly into this world, so that humans might be transformed, healed, and made whole. The presence of God became manifest in the words, the gestures, and the bodies of the believers. In this form of African-American worship the divine was embodied in the faithful. The emotional ecstasy of the slaves' worship expressed their profound belief that the preeminent place of God's presence in this world is the person. His altar is the human heart. Moreover, it is the whole person, body as well as spirit, that makes God present. In religious worship—dance, prayer, sermon, and song—the human person, embodied spirit and inspirited body, became an icon of God. A radically personal vision of life flowed from this kind of liturgy. Christian slaves fought off slavery's terrible power to depersonalize its victims by experiencing themselves as images of the divine. Anything, then, that defaced this human image of God was sacrilegious.

In addition to the communal experience of worship, the individual slave's experience of conversion effectively reaffirmed the dignity and worth of the slaves as children of God. Events of great spiritual power, conversions involved a deep reorienting of the values and direction of the convert. The life of the individual slave became part of the age-old struggle between good and evil, a drama of cosmic importance. Slaves spoke of conversion as an experience of rebirth, of being made entirely new, of being filled with love for everything and everybody. To experience, as they did, the unconditional love of God shattered the mentality of slavery. They realized—and realized with the heart not just the head—that they were of infinite worth as children of God. The conversion experience grounded their significance in the unimpeachable authority of almighty God, no matter what white people thought and taught. They knew that they constituted, what James Baldwin called, "a spiritual aristocracy," family members in the long genealogy of prophets, apostles, saints, and martyrs made up of those who did not simply talk about God, but experienced His power upon the altars of their hearts. "We be holy; you not be holy," as a group of slaves remarked to their mistress after their conversion. We might expect that their identification with the biblical children of Israel, with Jesus, the suffering servant, and with the saints and martyrs of Christian tradition might have pushed the slaves toward self-righteousness and racial chauvinism. Instead, it inspired compassion for all who suffer, even, occasionally for their white oppressors. William Grimes, for example, a slave who refused to lie or to steal, was unjustly accused and punished by his master. "I forgave my master in my own heart for all this, and prayed to God to forgive him and turn his heart," Grimes reported.[68] Mary Younger, a fugitive slave who escaped to Canada, remarked: "if those slaveholders were to come here, I would treat them well, just to shame them by showing that I had humanity."[69] When slaves forgave and prayed for slaveholders, they not only proved their humanity, they also displayed to an heroic degree their obedience to Christ's command: "Love your enemies. Do good to those who persecute and spitefully use you."

## Compassion

Out of the religion of American slaves a music arose that constituted one of this nation's most significant contributions to world culture. This music spread the message of the slaves' religious legacy far and wide. People around the world have been moved by the capacity of slave spirituals to take the particular suffering of black people in America and extend it into a parable of universal human experience. Gandhi spoke for many when he remarked to Howard and Sue Bailey Thurman that the spirituals got to "the root of the experience of the entire human race under the spread of the healing wings of suffering."[70] What meaning can we glean from the slaves' suffering?

There is no virtue in suffering for its own sake. To romanticize suffering, poverty, and oppression—as affluent Americans sometimes do—trivializes injustice and leaves unchanged the conditions that cause suffering. Conversely to shun suffering at all costs is futile. Suffering is an inescapable part of the human condition for masters, as well as slaves, for the rich, no less than the poor. On this human existential level, the slave experience teaches us that suffering must be lived through; it can't be avoided by any of the spurious means of escape that people use to distract one another from real life. Life as it is is bittersweet, joyful sadness. Unless we realize and accept our radical contingency, our mortality, we succumb to illusion, the illusion that we are omnipotent, that we are in control of our lives. We feed this illusion by preoccupying ourselves with an ever-spiraling cycle of needs, pretending that we have no needs that we cannot ourselves meet, in a vain attempt to deny our suffering and death. These illusions of power become dangerous when we try to live them out by exercising power over others. This deformation of our humanity takes on exceptional force because it is driven by a deep, usually unconscious, fear. The vicious cycle of need, gratification, need that drives modern consumer culture, distracts us from facing our fear of suffering and death. The spirituals, as Gandhi and others appreciated, speak of an alternative. They reveal the capability of the human spirit to transcend bitter sorrow and to resist the persistent attempts of evil to strike it down.

Moreover, Christianity taught the slaves that God had entered into the world and taken on its suffering, not just the regular suffering of all creatures that grow old and die, but the suffering of the innocent persecuted by the unjust, the suffering of abandonment and seeming failure, the suffering of love offered and refused, the suffering of evil apparently triumphant over good. They learned that God's compassion was so great that He entered the world to share its brokenness in order to heal and transform it. The passion, death, and resurrection of Jesus began and effected the process of that transformation. It was compassion, the love of all to the extent of sharing in their suffering, that would continue and bring to completion the work of Christ. All of this of course is paradoxical. All of this is of course a matter of faith.

American slaves accepted that faith. And in doing so they found their lives transformed. No, the suffering didn't stop. Many died still in bondage. And yet, they lived and died with their humanity intact, that is, they lived lives of inner freedom, lives of wisdom and compassion. For their condition, evil as it was, did not ultimately contain or define them. They transcended slavery because they believed God made them in His image with a dignity and value that no slaveholder could efface. When white Christians desecrated the gospel by claiming that it supported racial slavery, they defended true Christianity against this false heresy, even at the risk of their lives.

Reflecting theologically upon their experience of suffering as a people, African-Americans came to believe that those who oppress and enslave others, those who spread "civilization and the gospel" by conquest, those who degrade other races, those who turn Christianity into a clan religion, have already been condemned. Whereas, those who were oppressed but did not oppress, those who were enslaved but did not enslave, those who were hated but did not hate, have already entered the kingdom of the One who judges us all according to the measure of our compassion. "As long as you did it to the least of these, you did it to me."

Toward the end of her life, ninety-year-old former slave, Maria Jenkins, replied to an interviewer who asked her if all her people were dead: "De whole nation dead," she said. "De whole nation dead—Peggy dead—Toby dead—all leaning on de Lord." We know that the dead are not gone. They are here with us, a cloud of witnesses: Peggy, Toby, Charlotte Martin and her brother, Candace Richardson, Lucretia Alexander, Henry Bibb, Andrew and Sampson Bryan, Richard Carrothers and many, many more. They are here with us. O slave martyrs, confessors, and passion bearers, pray to God for us.

# 8

## THE CALL OF
## THE RIGHTEOUS
## SLAVE CONFESSORS

### FR. DAMASCENE CHRISTENSEN

EVERY NATION HAS ITS OWN "canopy of grace," a store-house of divine energy gathered from the sufferings and prayers of all those of that nation who have lived and died in devotion to Christ. This canopy acts as a protecting influence on the nation, and this energy can be tapped by the nation's people at any time, if only they will love and value the sufferings of their Christian forebears.

In the United States of America, we have a special canopy of grace arising from the righteous Christian African-American slaves, who are now in heaven praying for us. Their miraculous Christian witness is almost entirely overlooked by our contemporary society, both black and white, both Orthodox and non-Orthodox. The purpose of this talk will be to place their martyric experience in its proper, universal, Orthodox perspective, to reveal its spiritual significance, and to show how it can be applied to our lives today, as Christians living in the United States at the time of its moral collapse. In so doing, we wish to help Americans enter into the depth of this experience and tap to the full from the American repository of sanctity.

### True Christianity

In looking at the testimony of the righteous slaves from the Orthodox Christian world-view, we'll be exploring many different angles: theological, philosophical, historical, and even psychological.

By "the Orthodox world-view," I do not mean merely a particular expression of Christianity arising from certain cultures. Orthodoxy is universal Truth. It embraces all that is true, wherever it may be, and rejects all that is false. It is the fullness of Christ's revelation; and Christ's revelation is the fullness of God's revelation to the human race.

According to the Orthodox world-view, the experience of black Americans under slavery was an expression of the very essence of Christianity: the most profound expression of it in America outside the formal limits of the ancient Orthodox Church herself. Although the slaves were not directly exposed to Orthodoxy, they became much more Orthodox in spirit than the white people who introduced them to Christianity. They are a bridge to true, otherworldly Christianity here in America: a bridge that leads ultimately to the Orthodox Church.

True Christianity is the taking on, in oneself, of the radical commandments of Jesus Christ, such as, "He who hates his life in this world will keep it unto life eternal"; "If any one will come after me, let him deny himself, and take up his cross and follow me. For whoever will save his life will lose it; and whoever will lose his life for my sake will find it"; "If the world hates you, you know that it hated me before it hated you. If you were of the world, the world would love its own; but because you are not of the world, but I have chosen you out of the world, therefore the world hates you. If they have persecuted me, they will also persecute you"; and "Blessed are the poor in spirit: for theirs is the kingdom of heaven. Blessed are they that mourn, for they shall be comforted. . . ."

True Christianity does not accommodate itself to this world; it is not utilized for the sake of worldly benefit. Rather, it is founded on suffering in this world: not meaningless, dumb suffering, but redemptive suffering in devotion to God. St. Mark the Ascetic (sixth century) said: "Remembrance of God is pain of heart endured in the spirit of devotion." Through this devotion in the midst of pain, there comes salvation. In the Orthodox understanding, salvation does not just mean going to heaven after we die. It means first of all deliverance from our sin-condition, so that we are inwardly transformed, free from anger, hatred, resentment, and other passions.

We speak here not of experiencing a temporary "spiritual" high, nor of taking on an outwardly Christian identity and becoming a "nice" person. Rather, we are speaking of a mystical transformation from the animal-life to the life of the spirit, when we find the Kingdom of God within us and live from that inward place, so that nothing on the outside can shake us. Only suffering and deep mourning over sin can lead us to that place. As we will later show, the American slaves entered that place; they found the essence of Christianity and the true meaning of salvation; and thus it was that they entered into the spirit, if not the outward form, of ancient, apostolic Orthodox Christianity.

As we have said, Orthodoxy, being the fullness of Truth, embraces all that is true, wherever it may be. Thus, it cannot but embrace the experience of the righteous African-American slaves and, in a mystical sense, call them her own.

## Orthodoxy and African-America

When I was growing up, I had some good experiences in modern Western Christianity—what has been called the "white man's religion"—but I felt there was something definitely lacking in it. It was outward, not inward; it lacked even the concept of a true mystical transformation; it was too fluffy and comfortable, having accommodated itself to the world and taken its lead from the world. So I turned away from it and started seeking elsewhere. My search led me first of all into the realm of Eastern religions, especially those of China and Japan. I became fairly involved in that, yet since the seeds of Christ's truth had been planted in me as a child, my soul was never fulfilled there. Jesus Christ, working in my soul, was continually calling me back to Him. I fell into a period of great despair even while I was practicing Eastern religions. And then I discovered Eastern Orthodoxy, which, although it was Christianity and had white people in it, was not the Western "white man's religion." It was different from anything I had experienced. It contained those elements that I had found lacking in the other churches.

The first Orthodox service I attended was the Canon of St. Andrew of Crete, during Great Lent. All the lights were out in the church, just the lampadas were burning; and they were reading verses written in the fifth century by St. Andrew. Each verse brought out an image from the Old Testament, and each was designed to lead the soul to repentance. Between each verse they would sing, in a plaintive melody, "Have mercy on me, O God, have mercy on me."

Here I saw a dimension of Christianity that I had never seen before, a profound ascetic, mystical and otherworldly dimension, based on redemptive suffering, repentance, and inward purification: the essence of Christianity. And so, after sorting out all my mental baggage, I embraced the Orthodox faith and began to enter into that essence.

It was only after this that I came to appreciate the experience of the African-American slaves, especially through their music, the Spirituals. I knew there was something unearthly about that music, which was Orthodox in its feeling, content, and pathos. It was not simply made by people sitting down and writing hymns; it was divinely inspired. I began to make an extensive study of it, which I presented at the annual Pilgrimage at our monastery in 1987. After that, the Ancient Christianity and African-America Conferences started, and others have given talks on the connection between Orthodoxy and the African-American experience.

When I began reading on this subject, I found little material written by people who had an Orthodox understanding of what really went on, spiritually speaking, under slavery in America. One of the best works I found was a book called *The Book of American Negro Spirituals* by James Weldon Johnson (1871-1938), a profound black Christian writer, poet and statesman. But I didn't find much else with the same depth.

Then recently, just a few days before the 1997 Conference, for which I was preparing a talk, a friend of mine who was doing research on the slave martyrs told me about a book he had found, a very good book on slave religion. I went to pick it up at his house and started reading it. I was quite struck by it, for it caught the essence of the slave experience from an Orthodox point of view. I looked at the picture of the African-American author at the back and saw that, at the time the book was published in 1978, he was a professor at UC Berkeley. I thought, "I'd like to meet that man some day, but I probably never will. I wonder where he is now, what he is doing, what his religious ideas are." Being excited about the book, I began to tell one of the monks at the monastery about it, saying it was the best book I had ever read on the subject. The monk asked who the author was, and I told him it was Albert J. Raboteau. "Oh," he said, "he's going to be at the conference. He's going to give a lecture. And I heard that he recently became Orthodox." I was stunned. For me, this was another vindication of my belief that the American slave experience leads to Orthodoxy.

## The Meaning of Suffering

In order to better understand the experience of the African-American slaves, we'll now examine briefly the universal principles of spiritual life, especially the principle of suffering.

Mankind was originally created by God in order to rise in love toward Him, to climb ever closer to Him. That's still man's designation. Man's spirit still has that innate longing for God.

When the primordial Fall occurred, man, instead of choosing the more arduous way of climbing towards God, chose what was closer and easier at hand: his body and his senses. The Holy Fathers say that all sins can be traced to two sources: self-love and sensual pleasure.

Thus man, instead of rising towards God, fell in love with himself, or more precisely his lower self, his animal nature. In so doing, he began to lose touch with the original nature common to all humanity; and that's why the first son of the first man, Cain, committed the first murder.

Before the Fall, there was no suffering in the world; there was only spiritual pleasure, only joy. After the Fall, God allowed suffering to enter the world not as a chastisement—for He has no need to see people punished—but out of love. If God would not have allowed suffering, there would have been nothing to check the spread of evil in the world. Man would get further and further entrenched in love of himself, seeking sensual pleasures for himself, growing in massive pride just like the devil, and we would all be like demons. God allowed suffering because, if it is met in the right way, it can lead to redemption, it can purify us. Suffering reminds us that we're moving away from our original designation and from the knowledge of who we are.

If we're involved in some sin—whether it's a sensual pleasure or a resentment against someone—we can feel a certain exhilaration from it, which makes us feel better and not so guilty. But eventually, through suffering, we're led back to the awareness that something is deeply wrong. Without suffering, there's no way we could find that out; we'd be completely blinded.

God cherishes freedom. In order to love Him and each other, we must have freedom to love or not love. There is no love without freedom. That's why God has created us free like He is; that's why He allows us to ravage the earth and inflict suffering on our fellow human beings. But in the midst of this suffering He wants to deliver any who call upon Him and wish to turn away from their fallenness, to return to their true designation. He accomplishes this return without meddling with man's freedom. He lets man make a mess of things and then in His omnipotence He uses this very mess to help man return to Him. Only God can do that. The devil, even while seeming to gain victory over a man's soul, often loses in his very victory, for God can turn it around and use the mess the devil created to bring the soul to Him through suffering.

## Repentance

Suffering, then, leads to repentance. In Greek the word for repentance is *metanoia*. *Noia* comes from the word *nous*, an Orthodox patristic term for which there is no adequate English translation. Sometimes it's translated as "mind," sometimes as "heart," sometimes as "the eye of the soul." The *nous* is our immortal spirit, the highest aspect of our soul, the "image of God" in us. It is of our original human nature; it's what makes us uniquely human. Of all the creatures on the earth, man alone possesses such a spirit, which is meant to know God, eternally commune with Him, and in Him alone find rest. Animals do not possess this spirit, although they do possess the lower aspects of the soul: consciousness, emotions, thoughts, and imagination.

*Meta* means to go beyond or to change. *Metanoia* or repentance, then, actually means to change one's mind and heart, to purify and illumine one's sick and darkened spirit and heal its wounds, to change the way one views reality by changing the very eye of the soul. As St. Macarius the Great says, "Christians have their own world, their own way of life, and mentality, and word, and activity. Quite different is the way of life, and mentality, and word, and activity of the men of this world. One thing is Christians, and another the lovers of the world; between the one and the other is a great separation."[71]

In *metanoia* born of suffering, a person starts to feel that there is something deeply wrong. He begins to grow sick of himself—not of his *nous,* not of his immortal soul, but of his fallen, unregenerate self. He begins to have a Godly self-hatred. When Christ said, "Hate your own life," He meant that we are to hate not the life given us by God, but rather the parasitical ego-life that attached itself to us when we began to follow the serpent's suggestions. In this self-hatred, we desire to change; and as our *metanoia* grows deeper we abandon ourselves completely to God. We see there's no use in seeking satisfaction from this earth. As Fr. Moses Berry's grandmother—the daughter of a former slave—used to tell him, "Never trust this world—it changes too fast."

Having tasted the misery of life without God, we want nothing in life other than to be with Him, to fulfill our spirit's purpose. As we have said, only suffering can lead us to this point. It can be any kind of suffering. It can be from a slavemaster; it can be from a communist torturer; it can be suffering from disease, from a prolonged illness; it can be emotional suffering from a fiancée or spouse who has left or a mother, father or child who has died. Also—and this is more often the case—it can be an internal, moral suffering over a sin we have performed or a state of sin we are in. It can arise from a state of judgment or resentment that eats us alive until at last we become sick of it, abandon everything and turn ourselves over to God. In any case, because *metanoia* cannot occur without suffering, suffering is necessary for our salvation.

Christ Himself suffered on the Cross and died for us. He did this in order to take away the sin of the world and blot out the curse that lay on all mankind, but in so doing He also set us an example of redemptive suffering. He said, "Follow me"; and after that, where did He go? He went to Calvary, to suffer and die on the Cross; and it was only afterwards that He resurrected and ascended into Heaven in triumph.

Through suffering and *metanoia*, a person becomes emptied. Emptied of his sinful self, the old man. Emptied so that he can be filled with God. Through Christ's sacrifice on the Cross, God grants forgiveness to all mankind, but only *objectively*. We must receive it subjectively through *metanoia*.

In the process of repentance, we finally begin to acknowledge our sins. When Adam fell he didn't do this. He basically blamed God, saying, "The woman whom *You* gave me, she gave me of the tree, and I ate." He could have stayed in Paradise if he had repented at that moment, but he didn't.

In repentance, we're reversing what Adam did. We're saying, "OK, God, I did it, it's my fault. Yes, she gave it to me but I took it. I wanted it and I ate it. I'm sorry, forgive me. I don't want anything else than to be with You." This must not just be said with the lips or in the mind; it must be experienced at the core of our being.

In repentance we stop running from ourselves and our own guilt. We face ourselves square on. When that happens, a miracle occurs in our soul. Our spirit actually changes. We become transfigured, and that experience is so real that we know Christ's forgiveness is real. We're no longer just reading in the Gospels about Christ forgiving sins: now it has actually happened to us. For those of us who have gone through this, it's the most real experience in our lives. Then and only then is a person truly free, whatever the circumstances of his or her life.

Repentance doesn't end. We must continually wash ourselves with repentance. That's why all Orthodox clergy and monastics are dressed in black, and why we have black in Church during Great Lent. People say, "Oh, why do you repent all the time, why are you constantly dwelling on your own sinfulness?" But that dwelling on our own sinfulness is the only source of joy. As Professor Raboteau has said, it's sorrow mixed with joy. Without that sorrow of repentance we have no joy. Without that repentance we're not free, we're always slaves. The minute we cease repenting, the minute we cease facing our sins, we are already becoming enslaved again.

## Forgiveness

Once the miracle of Christ's forgiveness has occurred in the soul, when one *knows* one has been forgiven by God, then another miracle occurs, and that is that *one will forgive everyone else,* even though they may be totally unworthy of forgiveness.

When we read about the Christian martyrs and confessors, including those under slavery in America and under atheist regimes in communist countries, we can see that it is not a human thing that they are able to forgive their torturers. It's superhuman, divine. You can't know the reality of that until you've tasted the essence of Christianity.

Tolstoy, the famous Russian writer, never really tasted that essence. He was dabbling in all sorts of other things. He always wanted to enter into the faith of the simple Russian peasant, but his pride prevented him. He said, "I love the things Christ says in the Gospels, but the one thing I just can't accept is that we are to love our enemies. That's humanly impossible." He's right, it *is* humanly impossible; it must occur in a supernatural way.

We begin to love our enemies by first going into ourselves and seeing our own sins. By finding our immortal spirit and allowing it to fulfill its true purpose—union with God—we find the one human nature common to all. And when we see how our own spirit is riddled with wounds, we see also how human nature itself is so wounded. We see our own sinfulness first, and then we see how all of human nature is wounded by sin. Thus, through repentance we have compassion for other wounded people, even if they be our own enemies and torturers. The saints went so deeply into this repentance that they could even say honestly that they felt themselves to be the most sinful people in the world. Without at all flinching in their confession of Christ's Truth, they could kiss the hands of their jailers, torturers and executioners.

The Orthodox Holy Fathers speak much about perfect love. Perfect love, they say, is not just a lot of love; it is not a matter of degrees. In the simplest terms, perfect love is *love for everyone equally,* based on a mystical apprehension of our common human nature. St. Maximus the Confessor writes: "Perfect love does not split up the one nature of human beings on the basis of their various dispositions, but ever looking steadfastly at this one nature, it loves all people equally. The one who has perfect love and has reached the summit of detachment knows no distinction between one's own and another's, between faithful and unfaithful, between slave and freeman, or indeed between male and female. But having risen above the tyranny of the passions and looking to the one nature of people, he regards all people equally and is equally disposed toward all. For in him there is neither Greek nor Jew [here we could add, neither black nor white], neither male nor female, neither slave nor freeman, but Christ is everything and in everything."[72]

This, then, is the very essence of Christianity which the African-American slaves entered into. It is what has been experienced in the Orthodox Church throughout the ages: the miracle of transformation in Christ through suffering and repentance, leading to perfect love and forgiveness.

## Catacomb Christianity in Ancient Times

During the first three centuries of Christianity, its mystical essence was nurtured and preserved in the catacombs, receiving there the principle of its development through suffering and persecution. Because Christianity was considered a threat to the pagan Roman religion, Christians had to hide in the sepulchral tunnels (catacombs) which extended for miles beneath the city of Rome, there to hold secret prayer services at scheduled times of the day and night. If caught, they faced torture and death at the hands of the Roman authorities. At any time they could be taken off to be torn apart in the arena by lions. Thus they lived in a constant state of watchfulness and prayer. Their whole souls were directed toward the other world, and at all times they lived in the presence of that world.

Ostracized from the society around them, constantly faced with gross injustices, suffering want, experiencing also the transience of this earthly life, the catacomb Christians had to know the essence of Christianity or else they could no longer be Christians. Their very suffering for Christ led to this knowledge, for in it they could repent and find the Kingdom of God within them. And out of that inward place came peace, love, joy and forgiveness.

In his article, "African Pillars of the Church," Fr. Jerome Sanderson gives a powerful image of what the early Christian martyrs and confessors were like. He describes the ancient women martyrs from Africa: Felicity, who even though she was still nursing her baby longed for and went to martyrdom for Christ; and also Perpetua, who wished for martyrdom even while she was pregnant. These women, like the thousands of other martyrs of ancient times, wanted nothing else than to be with their Savior. They had no expectation of anything in this world.

After Christianity was finally legalized in 313 A.D. and Christians came out of the catacombs, the catacomb experience was so precious to believers that thousands went out into the desert in order to continue a catacomb-like existence of suffering for Christ. They came to be called monks and nuns; and the monastic tradition that came out of this gave to the Orthodox Church the tenor of her spiritual life. That's why Orthodoxy has preserved the essence of Christianity: the repentance, the ascetic dimension, the interior life. The catacomb experience lies at the heart of Christianity. Our faith in its essence is catacomb.

## Catacomb Christianity Under Communism

Since through suffering we enter into the mystery of Christ and the Cross, true Christianity has always thrived in conditions of persecution. It is there that its greatest glory is always seen.

In the fourth century, the great Orthodox theologian, St. Gregory Nazianzen, described our faith as "suffering Orthodoxy," and so it has been throughout the whole history of the Church. Although the catacomb period of the Church ended in 313 A.D., her persecution by the world did not. First there was persecution by the early heretics, then by the Moslems, then by the Latinizers, and finally, in our own century, by the communists. All these waves of persecution produced martyrs and confessors, and in all of them believers entered into the meaning of catacomb Christianity.

The experience of the black Christian slaves in America is generally not seen in this historical catacomb context. As we will attempt to show, however, this experience was catacomb in nature, even though the fullness of historical Orthodox Christianity was not made available to the slaves.

In order to make our comparison more clear, we will turn first to some accounts of catacomb Christianity in our own century. We will see how the essence of Christianity was discovered in suffering and persecution under the slavery of communism, and then show how the same occurred under American slavery.

I'll refer first to the writings of Richard Wurmbrand, a Romanian Christian pastor who converted from Judaism and endured fourteen years of torture in communist prisons for preaching the Gospel. He's been here in America for many years doing missionary work to Christians suffering persecution under Islam and under communism. He tells many stories of the superhuman power of forgiveness exhibited by fellow prisoners who were Christians.

Before he was put in prison, Richard Wurmbrand attended a congress of Christian leaders that had been convened in the Romanian parliament building by the communists. Four thousand priests, pastors and ministers of all denominations attended, and chose Joseph Stalin as the honorary president of the congress. One after another, the Christian leaders stood up on stage and praised communism, saying how great the new government was, even though it was a godless regime that was killing off Christians. As these pastors were betraying Christ and the Truth, Richard Wurmbrand's wife (also a convert from Judaism) turned to him and said, "Richard, stand up and wash this shame from the face of Christ! They are spitting in His face!" He said to his wife, "If I do so, you lose your husband." She said, "I don't wish to have a coward as a husband."

"Then I arose," Wurmbrand recalls, "and spoke to this congress, praising not the murderers of Christians, but Christ and God and said that our loyalty is due first to Him. The speeches at this congress were broadcast and the whole country could hear proclaimed from the rostrum of the Communist Parliament the message of Christ. Afterward I had to pay for this, but it had been worthwhile."[73]

Wurmbrand's first prison term lasted eight and a half years. When he was released, he continued preaching the Gospel, for which he was put back in again. Here is what he said after fourteen years of unspeakable tortures:

> The prison years did not seem too long for me, for I discovered, alone in my cell, that beyond belief and love there is a delight in God: a deep and extraordinary ecstasy of happiness that is like nothing in this world. And when I came out of jail I was like someone who comes down from a mountaintop where he has seen for miles around the peace and beauty of the countryside, and now returns to the plain.[74]

In his books, Richard Wurmbrand tells of being frozen to within just one minute or two of death, then being thawed—and having this process repeated over and over again. Having described this and other horrible tortures, he says:

> This is only a very small part of what happened. Other things simply cannot be told. My heart would fail if I should tell them again and again. They are too terrible and obscene to put in writing.[75]

So he's never revealed to the world the worst tortures that he went through—systematic tortures which derive from twentieth-century psychology and technology, making the tortures of the ancient Romans and the nineteenth-century American slavemasters look primitive in comparison. But, incredibly, he says:

> I have seen Christians in communist prisons with 50 pounds of chains on their feet, tortured with red-hot iron pokers, in whose throats spoonfuls of salt had been forced, being kept afterward without water, starving, whipped, suffering from cold, and praying with fervor for the communists. This is humanly inexplicable! It is the love of Christ, which was shed into our hearts.
>
> Afterward, the communists who had tortured us came to prison, too. Under communism, communists, and even communist rulers, are put in prison almost as often as their adversaries. Now the tortured and the torturer were in the same cell. And while the non-Christians showed hatred toward their former inquisitors and beat them, Christians took their defense, even at the risk of being beaten themselves and accused of being accomplices with communism. I have seen Christians giving away their last slice of bread (we had at that time one slice a week) and the medicine which could save their lives to a sick communist torturer, who was now a fellow-prisoner.
>
> A Christian was sentenced to death. Before being executed, he was allowed to see his wife. His last words to his wife were, "You must know that I die loving those who kill me. They don't know what they do and my last request of you is to love them, too. Don't have bitterness in your heart because they kill your beloved one. We will meet in heaven."[76]

Richard Wurmbrand tells another story about a Romanian Orthodox Abbot named Iscu, who had been tortured mercilessly in prison by a young man named Vasilescu. Vasilescu had believed fervently in communism; but the communists—who like demons were constantly turning on each other—locked him up with the prisoners. Thus, Abbot Iscu was in prison with his torturer, and they were both bedridden, dying of tuberculosis. Richard Wurmbrand says:

> Vasilescu was sorry for himself now. He told me again and again of the terrible things he had done [the tortures he had inflicted] at the canal. He had not spared the Abbot. Vasilescu was obviously dying and I tried to give him a little comfort; but he couldn't rest. One night he woke up gasping for breath. "Pastor, I'm going," he said. "Please pray for me!" He dozed and woke again, and cried, "I believe in God!" Then he began to weep.
>
> At dawn Abbot Iscu called two prisoners to his bed and ordered, "Lift me out!"
>
> "You're too ill to move," they said. The whole room was upset. "What is it?" said voices. "Let us do it!"
>
> "Lift me out!" he repeated.

They picked him up. "To Vasilescu's bed," he said.

The Abbot sat beside the young man who had tortured him, and put a hand gently on his arm. "Be calm," he said soothingly. "You are young. You hardly knew what you were doing." He wiped sweat from the boy's forehead with a rag. "I forgive you with all my heart, and so would other Christians too. And if we forgive, surely Christ, who is better than us, will forgive. There is a place in Heaven for you, also." He received Vasilescu's confession and gave him Holy Communion, before being carried back to his bed.

During the night both the Abbot and Vasilescu died. I believe they went hand in hand to Heaven.[77]

Recently one of the nuns of our Brotherhood, Mother Nina, who had spent two years in Romania, went to visit another Romanian confessor and living martyr named Fr. George Calciu. He is an Orthodox priest now living on the East Coast, and is in his early 70's. He was imprisoned for twenty-two years, even longer than Richard Wurmbrand.

Fr. George was first arrested when he was only 21 years old. He was a medical student then, and although he had been raised in a pious Orthodox home in a Romanian village, his faith had not yet been tried by suffering.

During his first prison term, he was subjected to the experiment of Pitesti: the most diabolical system of torture ever devised. Its aim was to methodically and scientifically dismantle the human personality by making the victim betray all that he held dear, and then to remold the person according to the image of the communist "new man."

"There were four steps," recalls Fr. George in his interview with Mother Nina:

the installation of terror, the unmasking, the denouncement of other people, and, afterwards, the changing of our souls. These four steps were strictly thought out and planned. They had had long experience of this in Russia and were now bringing this experience to Romania.

There was no torture, moral and physical, that was not used. It is too humiliating and absolutely inhuman to tell you every torture. Too humiliating. You cannot imagine, to be completely naked and to be beaten and forced to submerge your head in a bucket of excrement. You cannot imagine. We never imagined that it is possible, you know. Only the devil could give images like that.

It was not the torture that was the most difficult problem, because they could torture you today, but tomorrow they had to torture someone else, so you had one or two days to rest. But you were always watched and forced to say bad things, blasphemy. They did not have

99

time to beat you every day, from morning until night. But they could force you to say something against your friend, something against God everyday. When you were tortured, after one or two hours of suffering, the pain would not be so strong, but after denying God and knowing yourself to be a blasphemer—that was the pain that *lasted*. Spiritual pain is more difficult to bear than bodily pain.

Without prayer, you cannot survive. . . . During the night, when everyone goes to bed, you gain your strength and you find your repentance. You pray for this. It is not complicated. You say, *"God, forgive me!"* It is enough! Just to say, "God, forgive me!" It is enough for your soul to regain its strength and to resist one day more and one day more and one day more. Not to die. Not to go crazy. Many of us went mad. But just to say, "God, forgive me," was like a shield. Just to say, "Forgive me, God." You knew very well that the next day you would again say something against God. But a few moments in the night, when you started to cry and to pray to God to forgive you and to help you, was very good.[78]

Mother Nina said that when Fr. George was telling her this, tears were streaming down his face. At one point she asked him how one retains one's human dignity in such humiliating situations. He replied:

I think before human dignity, is Christian dignity. Many times I forgot my human dignity. I was humiliated. I was insulted. But beyond this is Christian dignity: forgiveness and prayer for the other one. I remember when that one colonel came into my cell on Pascha, he was very angry with me, and he said: "I know that you are praying for me!" I said, "Yes, I do pray for you. I pray that God will forgive you. I pray that God will give you the light of His Resurrection." He was very angry. When I told him this he became even more angry with me because the devil in him wanted him to deny in his soul and mind that Jesus Christ *really* is resurrected. Many times it was a split between human dignity and Christian dignity. According to human dignity—as a human being or as a good man—it is very difficult to forgive. But it is not so very difficult for us, as Christians, to forgive. I do not deny human dignity, but I say that before it comes Christian dignity.

Sometimes when my human dignity failed, I became very angry with them. I was ready to ask God to punish them. I said, "God, they are Your enemies, not only mine. They are Yours, too." But as a Christian, I said, "Oh, God, forgive them. Give them the light of Your Resurrection."[79]

Through suffering in prison, and through meeting other Christians (especially priests) who were locked up with him, Fr. George discovered the reality of Jesus Christ and the Kingdom of Heaven within him, and he became transformed. By the time he was released, he had a burning desire to live and die for Christ. He became a priest and began to speak openly to hundreds of Romanian youth about the need for faith in God. He knew he would be arrested and thrown back into prison for this, but this time he was prepared:

> I was very well prepared for the second imprisonment, you know. Because I accepted prison and I fortified my soul with Liturgy, with prayers, with songs. I was very protected. I consider this second time in prison to be an expiation [an atonement]. God gave me the strength to resist. There was a collaboration between me and Jesus Christ before I went into prison.
>
> During my second time in prison I had a very strong desire to become a martyr. I wanted to die in prison. I was completely isolated from the world, even from my family. I loved them; I did not stop loving them, but it was like an exaltation. I wanted to become a martyr for Jesus Christ. He decided otherwise.[80]

Mother Nina said that, when she went to interview Fr. George, there was another woman there who had also gone through horrible experiences in communist Romania, but she couldn't talk about them. She became fearful at the mention of the subject, while Fr. George did not hesitate to talk about his entire life and give a lengthy interview. As Mother Nina explained, this was because Fr. George had repented, because he had known God's forgiveness and had forgiven everyone. Although he wept and still felt pain, he was a free man. "Now I am free," he told her. But the woman who was fearful had not forgiven. Thus, she was still bound, she was still a slave.

In speaking of the catacomb Christians under communism, I'll conclude by telling of the inward transformation that occurred in the soul of another Orthodox priest, Fr. Elias Chetverukhin:

> When he was arrested by the secret police and taken to prison in the far north in 1932, Fr. Elias found himself in such inhuman conditions that he began to despair. Deep in the night a groan burst out from his heart: "O Lord, why hast thou forsaken me? I served Thee faithfully, I gave my whole life to Thee. How fervently I served in church. After all my prayers to Thee, why am I so tormented?"
>
> The whole night he cried out thus. Then suddenly a divine visitation, like fire, touched the sufferer with unearthly consolation. When morning came he was a new man, as if he had been baptized with fire.
>
> After that night he could no longer live an ordinary life. When his wife was allowed to visit him two years later, he told her, "Do not think

that even if I get out I will ever serve as I did before. The old world is gone forever, and there is no return."

At their farewell he said, "You know, now I have come to burn intensely with love for Christ. Here I have come to understand that there is ultimately nothing better, nothing more wonderful than Him. I would die for Him!"

His wife set out on the long and difficult journey home. When she arrived a telegram was waiting for her. There had been a fire in the prison, and Fr. Elias had burned with eleven other men.

His very name, Elias, means "aflame."[81]

## The Catacomb Christianity of African-America

Now I'll cite some passages which show that the righteous American slaves experienced the same thing that we've been talking about in the ancient Christian Church and in our own century in the Catacomb Church.

Professor Raboteau has described how the slaves were often persecuted severely by their masters for praying and holding prayer meetings, and therefore they had to take their faith underground. As the catacomb Christians in ancient Roman times held secret prayer services in tunnels beneath the city, the American slaves held theirs in the fields, forests, thickets and swamps, out of reach of the patrols. And as in ancient catacomb times, the potential price for this was torture and death. Ex-slave Peter Randolph writes:

> In some places, if slaves are caught praying to God, they are whipped more than if they had committed a great crime. The slaveholders will allow the slaves to dance, but do not want them to pray to God. Sometimes, when a slave, on being whipped, calls upon God, he is forbidden to do so, under threat of having his throat cut, or brains blown out. Oh, reader! this seems very hard—that slaves cannot call upon their Maker, when the case most needs it. Sometimes the poor slave takes courage to ask his master to let him pray, and is driven away, with the answer that, if he is discovered praying, his back will pay the bill.[82]

In the same article, Randolph describes how he and other slaves would assemble to pray in the swamps:

> They have an understanding among themselves as to the time and place of getting together. This is often done by the first one arriving breaking boughs from the trees, and bending them in the direction of the selected spot.

In some cases the slaves became catacomb Christians in the literal sense, digging holes in the fields in which they hid and prayed. Another former slave, Ellen Butler, remembers:

Marster neber 'low he slaves to go to chu'ch. Dey hab big holes out in de fiel's dey git down in and pray. Dey done dat way 'cause de white folks didn't want 'em to pray. Dey uster pray for freedom. I dunno how dey larn to pray, 'cause dey warn't no preachers come roun' to teach 'em. I reckon de Lawd jis' mek 'em know how to pray.[83]

In the intensity of their communal devotion, the slaves' prayer meetings were like those of their ancient catacomb predecessors. As a former slave states, "Everyone's heart was in tune," and when they called on God out of heavy hearts, "they made heaven ring."[84]

Like the ancient catacomb Christians, the American slaves constantly experienced the imminence of death. Many slaves were beaten or worked to death in five to ten years. Some of the worst masters would think it was better to buy new slaves than to pay for medical treatment for the sick ones who were being worked to death.

Also, the Christian slaves of America were like the catacomb Christians in their sense of the transience of those things they held dear. Even slaves who had relatively good masters could—due to the financial insolvency or death of those masters—be sold again and snatched away from their loved ones—their parents and children—never to see them again.

Again, like the ancient catacomb Christians, the slaves were not considered citizens by the worldly society around them, and thus they were ostracized from the world.

## The African-American Experience of the Essence of Christianity

In suffering as did the catacomb Christians throughout history, the American slaves entered also into their experience of inward transformation. Here is a story from ex-slave Isaiah Jeffries. He's talking about the baptism and conversion of his mother:

When I got to be a big boy, my Ma got religion at de Camp meeting at El-Bethel. She shouted and sung fer three days, going all over de plantation and de neighboring ones, inviting her friends to come to see her baptized and shouting and praying fer dem. She went around to all de people dat she had done wrong and begged dere forgiveness. She sent fer dem dat had wronged her, and told dem dat she was born again and a new woman, and dat she would forgive dem. She wanted everybody dat was not saved to go up wid her. My Ma took me wid her to see her baptized, and I was so happy dat I sung and shouted wid her.[85]

This is an especially vivid example of how, when *metanoia* occurs in the soul, one naturally and immediately wants to ask forgiveness and to forgive everyone. Here is another account of a slave about his conversion:

I ran to an elm tree and tried to put my arms around it. Never had I felt such a love before. I just looked like I loved everything and everybody. The eyes of my mind were open, and I saw things as I never did before.[86]

This is what St. Paul calls the "renewing of the mind" (Romans 12:2), a level of spiritual understanding in which everything appears differently because one is now a different being on the inside. As we have said, one can now live from that inward place rather than living from the outside and reacting to outside pressures. That's why it becomes so easy to forgive.

"I'se saved," said one slave woman after her conversion. "De Lord done tell me I'se saved. Now I know de Lord will show me de way, I ain't gwine to grieve no more. No matter how much you all done beat me and my chillen de Lord will show me the way. And some day we never be slaves."[87]

This woman's daughter, Fanny Moore, relates "My mammy just grin all over her black wrinkled face" after she united herself to Christ. As a child in the hands of God, she could endure anything without being crushed by it, without resenting or even reacting. Fanny said that even when the cowhide lashes ripped the skin off her mother's back, she "just go back to de field singin."[88]

Here is another account of Christian forgiveness, from a man named Solomon Bayley who was in the same Methodist class meeting with the person who was going to sell his wife and infant daughter. He says:

To keep up true love and unity between him and me in the sight of God was extremely difficult. This was a cause of wrestling in my mind, but that scripture abode with me, "He that loveth father or mother or wife or children more than me is not worthy of me." Then I saw it became me to hate the sin with all my heart, but the sinner love. But I should have fainted if I had not looked at Jesus, the Author of my faith.[89]

Again, Tolstoy is right, it is humanly impossible to do that; but this slave knew that it was only possible through Jesus Christ.

Another source tells of a slave named Robert who escaped to the North:

> When asked whether the slaves if liberated would injure their masters—"cut their throats?" he replied, "No, I would rather kneel down and pray for my master than injure him." But, when asked how he felt when his master was knocked down by a colored man in Salem, to allow Robert time to escape, Robert paused a moment before his answer came: "Well, I will tell you the truth—I was glad he was knocked down, for that give me a chance to cut; but I did not want him hurt."[90]

This shows two things: first, that when people become Christians they don't just become docile; and secondly, that at the same time they have the superhuman power to forgive everything. Dr. Raboteau has pointed out that in Portugal they didn't want Christians as slaves because the Christians would run off into the woods. They wanted non-Christian slaves, because once you're a Christian you know that you have a human essence, an eternal spirit, the same as the slavemaster, the same as anyone else; that you are created in the image of God, and that you're a dignified human being before God no matter what. Fugitive slave John Hunter recalled:

> I have heard poor ignorant slaves, that did not know A from B, say that they did not believe the Lord ever intended them to be slaves, and that they did not see how it should be so.[91]

The indomitability of Christian faith is seen most beautifully in the story of a slave called "Praying Jacob." He had a rule of praying three times a day: at set hours of the day he would stop whatever he was doing and go and pray. His master, who was very cruel to his slaves, would point his gun at him and say that if he did not stop praying he would blow out his brains. But Jacob, having calmly finished praying, would tell the master that he was welcome to shoot: "Your loss will be my gain. I have two masters, one on earth and one in heaven—master Jesus in heaven, and master Saunders on earth. I have a soul and a body. The body belongs to you, master Saunders, and the soul to Jesus. Jesus says men ought always to pray, but you will not pray, neither do you want to have me pray."[92]

Praying Jacob did not regard his body as his self, for he knew what it meant to commune in his eternal spirit with his Creator. The slavemaster would rage half-drunk through the fields, whipping the

105

slaves, but he never dared to touch Jacob, for he feared the holy man's prayers. This is much like what Richard Wurmbrand said occurred in communist prisons, when torturers would drop their truncheons on beholding the faces of their Christian victims shining with unearthly light.

## The Power of Humility

Through the inner conversion of *metanoia,* the righteous slaves became truly humble, and in this humility lay their unearthly power. As the sixth-century Desert Father, Abba Dorotheus, said, "Nothing is more powerful than humility."[93] Nothing in the world, because nothing can break the truly humble person.

Humility is not docility. A person is truly humble when he does not rely at all on himself, but only relies on God. He is wholly *under* God, and knows that all his power comes from him. The proud person, on the other hand, relies on himself, and thus, even while seeming to wield personal power, is a weakling and a coward.

A heroic example of the power of humility is seen in Harriet Tubman (1820-1913), who escaped from slavery in the South. She came to be called the "Moses of her people" because she personally led over three hundred slaves from the South to freedom in the North along the route of the Underground Railroad. She kept going back to the South even though there was a tremendous price on her head. When asked how it was possible that she was not afraid, she would always answer:

> Why don't I tell you, Missus, t'want *me,* 'twas *de Lord!* I always *tole* Him, "I trust You. I don't know where to go or what to do, but I expect You to lead me." An' He always did.

When the Southern slaveholders raised the price on her head, and added various threats of the cruel devices by which she should be tortured and put to death, her friends in the North gathered around her, imploring her not to go back to the South in the face of such a death. But Harriet answered:

> Now look yer! John saw the city, didn't he? Yes, John saw the city. Well, what did he see? He saw twelve gates—three of dose gates was on de north—three of 'em was on de east—and three of 'em was on de west—but dere was three of 'em on de *South* too' an' I reckon if dey kill me down dere, I'll get into one of dem gates, don't you?[94]

One account tells how Harriet locked arms with a slave who had escaped to the North and was being taken manacled to jail. She held on tight while being jostled in the crowd and being beaten over the head with policemen's clubs:

> Again and again they were knocked down, the poor slave utterly help-less, with his manacled wrists streaming with blood. Harriet's outer clothes were torn from her, and even her stout shoes were all pulled from her feet, yet she never relinquished her hold of the man, till she had dragged him to the river, where he was tumbled into a boat, Harriet following in a ferryboat to the other side.[95]

## Fate Beyond the Grave

As Professor Raboteau observes in his book *Slave Religion,* the slaves, no matter what they were taught about their inferior position, knew that they were, spiritually speaking, in an infinitely better condition than the whites who oppressed them. This knowledge was borne out by plain manifestations of the slaveholders' guilt and ultimate condemnation. Ex-slave John Brown recalls his master's death-bed attempt to save his soul:

> There was my old master Thomas Stevens. Ever so many times before his time was come. But though he recovered from his illnesses, in his frights he sent for us all and asked us to forgive him. Many a time he would exclaim that he wished "he'd never seen a nigger." I remember his calling old Aunt Sally to him and begging and praying of her to get the devil away from behind the door, and such like.
>
> It is a common belief amongst us that all the masters die in an aw-ful fright, for it is usual for the slaves to be called up on such occa-sions to say they forgive them for what they have done. So we come to think their minds must be dreadfully uneasy about holding slaves.[96]

On becoming Christians, the slaves knew that those who perse-cuted them would suffer immeasurably more than they themselves did, and eternally. They saw that their masters were destroying their own souls, while they themselves were being prepared for Paradise through suffering. This again made it easy to forgive, to follow Christ's commandment: "Love your enemies, bless them that curse you, do good to them that hate you, and pray for them which de-spitefully use you and persecute you."

## The First Miracle: Learning True Christianity from God Directly

When we look at the lives of these slave confessors we see three miracles. The first miracle is that they became Christians at all. Only the fact that Christianity is the Truth and that Christ is real could account for them becoming Christians. According to human reasoning they should have rejected it since it was the religion of their oppressor, and besides, they were taught a distorted and prostituted form of it. Ex-slave Charlie Van Dyke recalls:

> Church was what they called it but all that preacher talked about was for us slaves to obey our masters and not to lie and steal. Nothing about Jesus was ever said, and the overseer stood there to see the preacher talked as he wanted him to talk.[97]

Basically, these white preachers were doing the same thing that the pastors in communist times did, when, as at the conference described by Richard Wurmbrand, they praised the atheist government and distorted the Gospel for the sake of worldly advantage.

Ex-slave Peter Randolph relates:

> There was one Brother Shell [a white minister] who used to preach. One Sabbath, while exhorting the poor, impenitent, hard-hearted, ungrateful slaves, so much beloved by their masters [here Randolph is being facetious], to repentance and prayerfulness, while entreating them to lead good lives, that they might escape the wrath (of the lash) to come, some of his crocodile tears overflowed his cheek. . . . But, my readers, Monday morning, Brother Shell was afflicted with his old malady, hardness of heart, so that he was obliged to catch one of the sisters by the throat, and give her a terrible flogging.
>
> The like of this is the preaching, and these are the men that spread the Gospel among the slaves. Ah! such a Gospel had better be buried in oblivion. Such preachers ought to be forbidden by the laws of the land ever to mock again the blessed religion of Jesus, which was sent as a light to the world.[98]

Nevertheless, despite these hireling shepherds, the slaves not only embraced Christianity; they entered into the heart of it and became true Christians where their masters did not.

St. Maximus the Confessor once said, "He who knows the mystery of the Cross and the Tomb, knows also the secret essences of all things."[99] The slaves knew that mystery, for they bore the Cross along with Christ and they entered the Tomb with Him. As they suffered in devotion to Christ, their spiritual eyes were opened and they beheld the inner nature of reality. That is why they could say, "I saw things as I never did before." Moreover, that is why, when the white ministers preached to them a distorted Gospel, they could instantly discern the lie in it, and could separate that from the Truth hidden between the lines of what they heard.

Most of the slaves could not read the Bible. If they were caught learning how to read and write, they were often whipped and in some cases their fingernails were pulled out. Nor were they exposed to ancient Orthodox Christianity. All that most of them had available to them was eighteenth- and nineteenth-century Protestantism, which—even at its best, without the distortions added by the slave-masters—was cut off from the line of ancient Christian tradition.

But God is not limited; He can do anything He wills. As Christ said, "God is able of these stones to raise up children unto Abraham." He can raise a person to sanctity through direct intervention. When He sees a human soul that is suffering, having no earthly consolation and calling out to Him, He's not going to withhold his grace. He's going to give maximum, He's going to totally flood that person with grace. That's what He did to these slaves, who were converted in their hearts on the spot.

The slave narrative of Josiah Henson gives an especially vivid portrayal of how the meaning of Christ's Cross and redemptive suffering penetrated immediately into the hearts of the slaves. Henson speaks of going to a prayer meeting for the first time when he was 18 years old, having never before heard a sermon or any discourse on religious topics:

> When I arrived at the place of meeting . . . the speaker was just beginning his discourse, from the text, Hebrews 2:9, "That He, by the grace of God, should taste of death for every man." This was the first text of the Bible to which I had ever listened, knowing it to be such. I have never forgotten it, and scarce a day has passed since, in which I have not recalled it, and the sermon that was preached from it. . . . I was wonderfully impressed with the use which the preacher made of the last words of text, "for every man." He said the death of Christ was not designed for a select few only, but for the salvation of the world, for the bond as well as the free; and he dwelt on the glad tidings of the Gospel to the poor, the persecuted, and the distressed, its deliverance to the captive, and the liberty wherewith Christ has made us free, till my heart burned within me, and I was in a state of the greatest excitement at the thought that such a being as Jesus Christ had been described should have died for me. . . . I immediately determined to find out something more about Christ and His being crucified, and revolving the things which I had heard in my mind as I went home, I became so excited that I turned aside from the road into the woods, and prayed to God for light and for aid with an earnestness which the subsequent course of my life has led me to imagine might not have been unacceptable to Him who heareth prayer.[100]

The miracle of the slaves' conversion is undeniably evident especially in those cases when they received the Gospel not from other people, but from God directly. I'll cite some testimonies of this from the slaves themselves.

Here's a man talking about how he became a preacher:

> Yer see I am a preacher. De Lord call me once when I was workin'. He call me and told me, in imagination, you know, that He wanted me to preach. I told him I didn't know enough, that I was ig'nant, and the folks would laugh at me. But He drew me on and I prayed. I prayed out in the woods, and every time I tried to get up from my knees He would draw me down again. An' at last a great light came down sudden to me, a light as big as the moon, an' struck me hard on the head and on each shoulder and on the bress here, here and here and here. . . . And den same time warm was in around my heart, and I felt that the Book was there. An' my tongue was untied, and I preach ever since and is not afraid. I can't read de Book, but I has it here, I has de text, and de meanin', and I speaks as well as I can, and de congregation takes what the Lord gives me.[101]

One of our monks noticed something amazing about this account. This preacher spoke of God making the sign of the Cross over him, in Orthodox fashion! Though living in a place where Orthodoxy was unknown, he was taught it by God Himself.

After they were free, the slaves were taught to read. They had tremendous veneration for the Bible, and wanted to learn how to read specifically so that they could read the Bible. But the old generation of slaves was very concerned by the new generation that was coming up, because the latter was being converted *through* the Bible, through outward learning. The old generation said, "That's not how we were converted!" Instead, they were converted through *metanoia,* through going out into the fields and "praying it out." At prayer meetings, they were not allowed to join the congregation until they were inwardly transformed. In the meantime, they had to weep over their sins on the "mourners' bench," which could go on for weeks, months, or even years. Only when the elders found their repentance and transformation genuine were they allowed to be baptized and join the ranks of true Christians.

Real conversion is not just catechism: it has to be deeper, and the righteous slaves knew that. They also said that their masters and their masters' families were "Bible Christians," and they did not want to be like them. Again, they had absolute reverence and love for the Bible, but they knew that salvation came not through memorizing verses and chapters, but through inner transformation. One ex-slave woman exclaimed:

Oh! I don't know nothing! I can't read a word. But, oh! I read Jesus in my heart, just as you read him in de Book. O, . . . my God! I got Him! I hold Him here all de time! He stay with me![102]

Here's one of the most striking examples of how the slaves learned the Christian faith directly from God. An ex-slave says:

God started on me when I was a little boy. I used to grieve a lot over my mother. She had been sold away from me and taken a long way off. One evening I was walking along thinking about Mama and crying. Then a voice spoke to me and said, "Blessed art thou."[103]

He was taught the Beatitudes directly. He didn't know anything about Scripture, he had no theology; but he was weeping, and God had mercy on him, spoke in his heart and taught him the Scripture, "Blessed are those who weep." This is reminiscent of the story of the sixth-century African saint, Mary of Egypt, who went out to live in the desert right after her conversion, with no chance to learn the Scripture, yet who came to know the Bible by heart through God's revelation.

## The Second Miracle: The Spirituals

The second miracle of the American slave experience is the creation of the Spirituals. In the 1920's James Weldon Johnson wrote:

As the years go by and I understand more about this music and its origin, the miracle of its production strikes me with increasing wonder. It would have been a notable achievement if the white people who settled in this country, having a common language and heritage, seeking liberty and a new land, faced with the task of conquering untamed nature, and stirred with the hope of building an empire, had created a body of folk music comparable to the Negro Spirituals. But from whom did these songs spring—these songs, unsurpassed among the folk songs of the world and, in the poignancy of their beauty, unequalled? . . . This music, which up to this time is the finest distinctive artistic contribution America has to offer the world. It is strange! I have termed this music noble, and I do so without qualifications. Take, for example, *Go Down Moses;* there is not a nobler theme in the whole musical literature of the world. If the Negro had voiced himself only in that one song, it would have been evidence of his nobility of soul. Add to this, *Deep River, Stand Still Jordan, Walk Together Children, Roll Jordan Roll, Ride On King Jesus,* and you catch a spirit that is a little more than a mere nobility; it is something akin to majestic grandeur. The music of these songs is always noble and their sentiment is always

exalted. Never does their philosophy fall below the highest and pur-
est motives of the heart. And this might seem stranger still.[104]

A highly cultured man, James Weldon Johnson was able to appreciate the Spirituals in relation to the Classical cultures of the world.
In his poem "O Black and Unknown Bards," he wrote:

Not that great German master [J. S. Bach] in his dream
Of harmonies that thundered amongst the stars
At the creation, ever heard a theme
Nobler than "Go down, Moses." Mark its bars . . .

There is a wide, wide wonder in it all,
That from degraded rest and servile toil
The fiery spirit of the seer should call
These simple children of the sun and soil.
O black slave singers, gone, forgot, unfamed,
You—you alone, of all the long, long line
Of those who've sung untaught, unknown, unnamed,
Have stretched out upward, seeking the divine.

You sang far better than you knew; the songs
That for your listeners' hungry hearts sufficed
Still live, —but more than this to you belongs:
You sang a race from wood and stone to Christ.[105]

Johnson's appraisal of the Spirituals as America's highest artistic
contribution to the world is generally acknowledged. John and Alan
Lomax, who are considered the main authorities on American folk
music, have written:

Whatever their origin, whatever their structure, whatever their com-
ponents—there can be no question in the minds and hearts of those
who have heard them that in the Negro Spirituals American folk art
reaches its highest point. Indeed, we assert that these songs form the
most impressive body of music anywhere on this earth.[106]

When Africans first came to this continent, not only could they
not speak or read English, but they could not even speak to each
other, for they had been taken from different tribes with different
languages. When they first began to gather to worship God, their
first spiritual songs were just wordless moans filled with profound
devotion, which they sent up to God in their pain. Then, to these
wordless songs, they began to add words. In the beginning, the only
words they used were, "Lord, have mercy," which they repeated over
and over again from the depth of their souls. No one taught them
this. They did not have Orthodox missionaries teaching them the
Jesus Prayer from the *Philokalia* ("Lord Jesus Christ, have mercy on

me"), but they, on their own, apprehended the essence of the Jesus Prayer. This can be seen as America's only natural apprehension of the Jesus Prayer. And again, this came out of suffering, just as the Jesus Prayer itself came out of suffering Orthodoxy.

After the emancipation of the slaves, when the folklorists began writing down the Spirituals, they found a girl who remembered one they had never heard before. They asked her where she had learned it. She said she had heard her father sing it to console himself after he had been whipped by his master or his master's men. Her father, she said, would sit there with lowered head, singing this song in tears, covered with blood. The words went like this, "I'm troubled, I'm troubled, I'm troubled in mind. If Jesus don't help me, I will surely die." This is a very poignant example of how these Spirituals were forged in blood.

Those who composed the Spirituals understood the meaning of the Beatitudes, which is the endurance of tribulation while retaining faith, devotion and inward joy. This is nowhere expressed more perfectly and succinctly than in these lines of a Spiritual: "Nobody knows the trouble I see, Nobody knows my sorrow, Nobody knows the trouble I see: Glory, Hallelujah." One of the most profound of all the Spirituals is *They Crucified My Lord,* also called *The Crucifixion.* It speaks of Christ's Passion, the nails, the spear, the blood trickling down, and it says at the end of every stanza: "An' He never said a mumbalin' word." The melody is solemn and dirge-like, descending on a melody line welling with tears. In listening to it we are moved by how intimately the slaves shared in Christ's Passion. They saw how truly noble it was that Christ never said a mumbling word, when, by all the laws of this world, He should have been filled with wrath instead of forgiveness. The fact that cruelly abused slaves produced a song like this is proof in itself that something above nature is at work in the Spirituals.

Roland Hays, who was a singer of the Spirituals and a transmitter of black American Christian culture, has written: "You may search the entire collection of black American folk songs extant, which number in the hundreds, and you will not find one word of hate or malice anywhere."

## The Third Miracle: Freedom

The third miracle in the African-American slave experience is the miracle of their freedom. The slaves knew that they would one day be free. Their inward Christian faith taught them that they *should* be free, and they were confident that God would deliver them. So they were constantly praying for deliverance. It was like a spiritual army. That army of praying slaves was really what brought down the whole institution of slavery. Ex-slave Tom Robinson recalled:

> I can just barely remember my mother. I was not eleven when they sold me away from her. But I do remember how she used to take us children and kneel down in front of the fireplace and pray. She'd pray that the time would come when everybody could worship the Lord under their own vine and fig tree—all of them free. It's come to me lots of times since. There she was a-praying. All over the country the same prayer was being prayed. Guess the Lord done heard the prayer and answered it.[107]

Another former slave, Clayborn Gantling, remembered:

> The slaves were sold in droves like cows. White men wuz drivin' 'em like hogs and cows for sale. Mothers and fathers were sold and parted from their chillun; they wuz sold to white people in diffunt states. I tell you chile, it was pitiful, but God did not let it last always. I have heard slaves morning and night pray for deliverance. Some of 'em would stand up in de fields and bend over cotton and corn and pray out loud for God to help 'em and in time you see He did.[108]

How could God not hear and respond to such prayer?

The masters, of course, didn't want the slaves to pray because they knew they would be praying for freedom. The whites sensed that the slaves' prayers had power. The white minister C. C. Jones, for example, felt put to shame by the powerful prayers said by Dembo, a native African who was a member of Jones' church:

> I can never forget the prayers of Dembo. There was a depth of humility, a conviction of sinfulness, an assurance of faith, a flowing out of love, a being swallowed up in God, which I never heard before nor since; and often when he closed his prayers, I felt as weak as water, and that I ought not to open my mouth in public, and indeed knew not what it was to pray.[109]

Ex-slave Rebecca Grant's account of her mother describes a depth of prayer and a level of sanctity that was not uncommon among the suffering slaves:

> My mother, all de time she'd be prayin' to de Lord. She'd take us chillun to de woods to pick up firewood, and we'd turn around to see her down on her knees behind a stump, a-prayin'. We'd see her wipin' her eyes wid de corner of her apron—first one eye, den de other—as we come along back. Den, back in de house, down on her knees, she'd be a-prayin'.[110]

The slavemasters sensed that the people they were oppressing were the very people about whom Christ spoke in the Beatitudes, "Blessed are the meek, blessed are those who weep, blessed are those who mourn," and about whom the Prophet David spoke in the Psalms, "A broken and a contrite heart, O God, Thou wilt not despise." They sensed that God was hearing those slaves and not them, which made them whip the slaves even harder for praying.

The tremendous value that the masters placed on the prayers of the slaves was especially seen when the Northern army was advancing on the South. The masters argued, begged, coaxed, threatened and punished the slaves to make them pray for the Confederates. One slave recalled:

> We pray for de war [that is, for the victory of the North]. Massah say we shouldn't, mus' pray for the 'fed'rates. We pray mo', pray harder. Den dey wouldn't let we hab meetin's, broke up de meetin's, but didn't broke our hearts, we pray mo' and mo', in de heart, night and day, and wait for de Lord. Oh, we pray for de Lord to come, to hasten His work.[111]

One account tells about how, when the Northern army was advancing, one of the plantation mistresses told the slaves, "Get together and pray that the Northern army be driven back." And so the slaves got together and prayed, "Lord, may Thy will be done." Then the Northerners continued advancing, and the South was losing the war; so the mistress told the slaves, "Wait a minute, what have you been praying for? It's not working." They said, "We've been praying that the Lord's will be done." She said, "Don't pray for *that*, pray that the Northern army will be driven back." "Well," they said, "if God wants the Northern army to be driven back, it will be driven back."[112]

All the while the slaves had a radical trust in God that His will *would* be done. After the war, an ex-slave told someone from the North:

> I knew God would bless you an' give victory. I feel it when I pray. Massah angry 'cause I pray for de North, can't help it, mus' pray for the whole worl'. Massah say, "No! Pray for de 'fed'rates." But I knew God would bless the North.[113]

The miracle of the slave's means of emancipation was seen most plainly in the way in which God raised up from among the common people an *unearthly man* in order to free them. That man was Abraham Lincoln.

Nowadays it's become unfashionable to speak of the greatness of

Abraham Lincoln. Young people in our schools are taught that his motives are suspect, that he didn't really care about the slaves, that all he really wanted to do was to save the Union. They're told that the Civil War was fought over politics and states' rights, and that slavery was the side-issue. This only shows how far our society has departed from a basic understanding of truth and righteousness. It's the exact *opposite* of the truth. When we view Lincoln and the Civil War from a spiritual point of view, we see that—as in everything else—the political issues were only the veneer, and that underneath them was the real battle which goes on all the time between good and evil, truth and falsehood, God and the devil. The real, spiritual issue was the evil of slavery, and states' rights was only the surface political issue. Lincoln was well aware of this, as can be clearly seen from his second inaugural address, which he gave during the Civil War, five months before he was killed. "One eighth of the whole population," he said, "were colored slaves, not distributed generally over the Union, but localized in the Southern part of it. These slaves constituted a peculiar and powerful interest. *All knew that this interest was, somehow, the cause of the war.*" Ultimately, the Civil War was fought over a moral idea.

In his early days, Lincoln had been somewhat of a freethinker; but during his presidency, and especially during the war, the tribulations with which he was assailed caused him to go deeply within himself, to seek out God and His holy will, and to try to view reality through God's eyes. This comes out in many of his statements and writings. In his second inaugural address we see him coming forth with a rigorously honest and profoundly spiritual view of the current upheavals. Speaking of the North and the South, he said:

> Both read the same Bible, and pray to the same God; and each invokes His name against the other. It may seem strange that any man should dare to ask a just God's assistance in wringing their bread from the sweat of other men's faces: but let us judge not that we be not judged. The prayers of both could not be answered; that of neither has been answered fully. The Almighty has His own purposes. "Woe unto the world because of offences! for it must needs be that offences come; but woe to that man by whom the offence cometh!" [Matt. 18:7]. If we shall suppose that American slavery is one of those offenses which, in the providence of God, must needs come, but which, having continued through His appointed time, He now wills to remove, and that He gives to both North and South this terrible war, as the woe due to those by whom the offense came, shall we discern therein any departure from those divine attributes which the believers in a Living God always ascribe to Him! Fondly do we hope—

fervently do we pray—that the mighty scourge of war may speedily pass away. Yet, if God wills that it continue, until all the wealth piled by the bondman's two hundred and fifty years of unrequited toil shall be sunk, and until every drop of blood drawn with the lash shall be paid by another drawn with the sword, as was said three thousand years ago, so still it must be said "the judgments of the Lord are true and righteous altogether" [Psalm 19:9].

With malice toward none; with charity for all; with firmness in the right, as God gives us to see the right, let us strive on to finish the work we are in; to bind up the nation's wounds, to care for him who shall have borne the battle, and for his widow and his orphan—to do all which may achieve and cherish a just and lasting peace, among ourselves, and with all nations.

In his sufferings, Lincoln too learned the essence of Christianity. Humble before God, he was not docile before evil, but stood firmly in what was right, all the while forgiving his enemies, not judging them, "having malice toward none." Thus he achieved true victory over evil. He did not seek to push his own will or a particular political agenda, but sought only the Truth, as God gave him to see it. Once someone asked him, "President Lincoln, do you believe that God is on the side of the North?" Lincoln replied, "What should matter to us is not whether God is on our side, but rather whether we are on God's side."

My Abbot, Fr. Herman, probably knows as much about Russian ascetics as anyone in the world, and has portraits of them all over his walls. One day he took me into his room and said, "Look at these pictures of Abraham Lincoln." It was a large book with sharp, clear photographic portraits of him taken at various periods of his life. Fr. Herman asked me, "Isn't that a picture of an ascetic?" And indeed, Lincoln's face, his sunken cheeks, the nobility of his expression, and especially the otherworldly look in his eyes were like those of all the ascetics whom Fr. Herman had on his walls.

A few years ago Fr. Herman and Fr. Moses (Berry) went to Lincoln's grave in Springfield, Illinois, and they were told by the person there, "When Lincoln's body was exhumed twenty years after his death, it was completely incorrupt." In the Orthodox Church, incorruption is a sign of sanctity; and many of the ascetics whom I've just mentioned were found to be incorrupt in precisely the same way. You can draw your own conclusion from this; but the point I wish to make here is that Abraham Lincoln was no ordinary man; he was a righteous, prophetic and martyric figure whom God raised in order to, like Moses, lead His enslaved people out of "Egypt-land" and into freedom. And this miracle occurred through the power of the prayers of the slaves. When he was a baby, when he was growing up, the slaves were praying for deliverance.

## An African-American Martyrology

We have just compiled a preliminary version of the African-American Martyrology (included as an appendix to this book).

At the 1996 Conference, when we were talking about the slave confessors, I said, "I know the slaves were whipped and tortured for praying, but I haven't found any documentation that they were actually killed for that reason. But if we could find a document about a single person who was killed, we could show that there were actually martyrs in the strictest sense of the word: people killed for holding prayer services and praying to Jesus Christ." When I said this, Matushka Michaila [Fr. Paisius' wife, who was raised by the sons and daughters of slaves in Arkansas] said, "My family told me that they were killed for praying. It happened!" And sure enough, in the past year we found accounts of this: two accounts of people who were actually killed, together with more accounts of those who were either beaten for praying or else confessed Christ in the midst of threats from their masters.

Christians throughout history have remembered the martyrs. "The blood of the martyrs is the seed of the Church." It is the foundation of the Church, because the martyrs bear witness to the reality of the other world, that Christ is real. From ancient times, Christians have nourished their souls with the lives of the martyrs. A believer would be killed in the arena, they would bring back his remains, and then they would serve Liturgy on the remains (relics). (Even today in the Orthodox Church, a priest must serve Liturgy on top of the bones of a martyr, which are sewn into the *antimens* covering the altar table.) They would paint the martyr's portrait (icon) on the walls of the catacombs, and they would tell and write down their stories (hagiography).

Suffering is the reality of the human condition. In traditional Christianity, people have been edified by hearing of those who suffered in this world with the hope of redemption, of being with Christ throughout eternity. Today, most Americans have lost this traditional source of edification: the inspiring tales of the strength and fearlessness of the martyrs amidst cruel tortures. And what has our modern society replaced them with? With horror movies! Movies and books which, instead of inspiring the soul toward heaven, instill in it infernal feelings which prepare it for hell. Our task as Orthodox Christians is to turn this situation around by holding up the American slave martyrs and confessors as heroes for ourselves and especially for our youth.

In the Orthodox Church there are three categories of martyrs and confessors. The first is comprised of *martyrs* who have died in confessing Jesus Christ. In the second category are the *confessors:* those who were tortured in confessing Christ, but who were not actually killed. They were those who wouldn't give in to slick Christianity, nor to the powerful of this world; who wouldn't accommodate their faith for worldly advantage. One of the greatest known confessors was St. Maximus the Confessor. His tongue was cut out because he was preaching the truth about the divine will and the human will of Christ. Many of these confessors actually wanted to be martyred, but God didn't grant that to them.

The third category is that of *passion-bearers.* These are believers who were not tortured or killed while confessing Christ directly, but who suffered or were killed in devotion to and love for Jesus Christ.

Of the men and women in our African-American Martyrology, so far we have records of two who qualify for the first category and eleven who qualify for the second category. Beyond this, there are records of hundreds of others in the third category, who can be called passion-bearers.

These records, of course, make up only a tiny fraction of the total number. As in Russia during the communist period, there are thousands of martyrs, confessors and passion-bearers whose names and stories have not come down to us. Our African-American Martyrology only scratches the surface of the whole phenomenon.

Orthodox Christians may object to our calling African-American slaves by the title of martyr, since a general criterion for Orthodox sainthood is baptism in the Orthodox Church. We will respond to this objection with two points. In the first place, there are many, many martyrs in the early Church who were not baptized Orthodox. They were pagans who, upon beholding the courageous sufferings of the martyrs, themselves confessed Christ and were immediately killed for this, before they had a chance to be baptized. Among them are Martyr Laodicius, who suffered alongside Martyr Glyceria in the year 141; Martyrs Alexander and Asterius, who suffered alongside Martyr Thaleleus in 284; and Martyrs Bacchus, Callimachus and Dionysius, who suffered alongside Martyr Barbarus in 362—to name only a few. The Church, in calling them martyrs, has affirmed that they were baptized in their blood.

In the case of the African-American martyrs, they of course cannot be blamed for not being Orthodox, since they never heard of Orthodoxy. As we have seen, however, they entered into the essence of true Christianity through their suffering, being taught it mystically by God. They were baptized into suffering Orthodoxy in their blood.

Since the American slave martyrs were never formally exposed to Orthodoxy, I would not advocate listing them in the universal Orthodox calendar of saints. Taking such a liberty could, as St. Paul says, "become a stumblingblock to them that are weak" (1 Cor. 8:9), and could open the door to all sorts of innovations regarding additions to the calendar. Nevertheless, I do believe that, as Orthodox Christians living in America, we should locally honor the American slave martyrs. We should hold them up as confessors and heroes for ourselves and especially for our youth. We can't expect any change in this country if we don't honor the very people in our own land who have confessed Christ: our own American martyrology.

Under the first category of martyrs, the first to be listed is Martyr Ezekiel. His master's father heard the slaves having a secret prayer meeting and heard Ezekiel praying that his master would change his heart and deliver him from slavery so that he may enjoy freedom. The next day Ezekiel (or Zeke, as they called him) disappeared. No one knew what happened to him. Then when the master's father was dying he told the white Baptist minister that he had killed Zeke for praying and that he was going to hell. That's how we know about his martyrdom.

Dr. Raboteau speaks of Charlotte Martin's brother, who was whipped to death for taking part in a prayer meeting. Not knowing his first name, we call him Martyr Martin.

In the second category, one of the most striking accounts is that of Sylvia Avery. Once more it shows the power and indomitability of these Christians.

Every morning Sylvia would pray, but the slavemaster despised this, saying the slaves were only praying so that they might become free. She would frequently get whipped for praying, but that did not stop her morning prayers. One morning, when Sylvia was pregnant, the master became so angry that he came to her cabin, pulled off her clothes, tied her to a young sapling, and whipped her so brutally that her body was raw all over. That night she crawled on her knees to the woods. For two weeks the master hunted for her but could not find her. When he finally did, she had given birth to twins. She lived to be 115 years old.

## What We Can Do

With the example of the slave martyrs and confessors before us, let us now ask what we ourselves can do. In response to this question, I have outlined five points.

1. *We as Christians have to know our own eternal soul, made in the image of God.* We have to know what's under our skin, to find the inner essence of who we really are. To do this we first have to know our own sins. When we go within and see the depths of sin in which we are living, then we will truly come to Jesus Christ as our Savior. As our Abbot often tells us, "Jesus Christ cannot be your Savior unless you know you are perishing, unless you know you are drowning." The slave martyrs knew they were perishing without Christ.

We come to Christ and we bear His cross gladly. He says, "My yoke is easy and my burden is light." Through our suffering with Him and knowing His forgiveness, our burdens surely do become light. In whatever kind of suffering God gives us, we can go through the process of *metanoia*. As the Spirituals say, we "go down to that lonesome valley."

You can't rise up, you can't be spiritually resurrected until you go down into that valley of suffering and repentance; until, as the righteous slaves used to say, you "pray it through." Only then will you know God's forgiveness. And knowing God's forgiveness, you can forgive everyone everything. Just like that slave we talked about, who said he wanted to hug that elm tree, to love everybody and everything. That's true Christianity. When you have entered into that experience, then you will not only know that you have an eternal soul within you, but you will also find the Kingdom of God within you. And having the Kingdom of God within you, you will seek and love God above all. St. Ignatius Brianchaninov says, "He who does not know the Kingdom of God within him will not recognize the spirit of anti-Christ." To this we could add that such a person will not be able to differentiate between slick Christianity and suffering Christianity, between worldly Christianity and otherworldly Christianity. When we know the Kingdom of God within us, we will seek to make our home, not in this world, but in the world to come.

2. Having gone through this painful inward transformation, we come to see the martyric suffering of the American slaves, endured in the spirit of devotion to Christ, not as a shame, but as *the glory of Christianity in this land.* It testifies to the redemptive power of Christ in the most deplorable conditions. And now that we see it as the glory of our American Christianity, we have a whole host of heroes for ourselves and especially for our youth.

3. *We honor our African-American martyrs and confessors;* we pray for the reposed righteous ones, as Fr. Moses Berry has said. We honor those who helped to bring about the end of the great sin of slavery in our land: the great abolitionists (both black and white), Abraham Lincoln, Harriet Beecher Stowe and others. But most of all we honor those slaves—those "prayer warriors"—who were unstoppable in their prayers and who, spiritually speaking, were the real ones responsible for the end of slavery.

4. We must remember that the enslavement, persecution and martyrdom of Christians is not just a thing of the past. More than an estimated 160,000 Christians were martyred in 1996, and countless others were subjected to unimaginable horrors at the hands of communist, Muslim, and other totalitarian regimes. Among the countries where this is taking place is Sudan in northern Africa. Jeff Jacoby, a columnist for the *Boston Globe,* writes:

> The Nuba mountains in Sudan, which have had a Christian population since the 6th century, are littered with mass graves. There have been reports of crucifixions of Christians by the army. Muslim troops from northern Sudan have sold tens of thousands of Christian children and women from the south into slavery. Many have been branded or mutilated to prevent escape; many more have been tortured, brainwashed or starved until they converted to Islam.[114]

It is our duty to *pray for these righteous sufferers.* How can we honor the Christian slave-martyrs and confessors of the past without also supplicating God for those in the present? Richard Wurmbrand's *Voice of the Martyrs Newsletter* provides a good source of information on current persecutions, and offers ways by which we can help.[115]

5. Finally, having undergone the transformation mentioned above, we *cease to resent.* This is a primary lesson from the American slave confessors and from their Spirituals. And it is a primary key of spiritual life, universal for every person.

Larry Elevtherios Johnson, an African-American convert to Orthodoxy, recalls:

> When I pressed my grandmother about the pain of segregation during her time, she would simply laugh. She would tell me to just "trust in God." I once pointedly asked her why our younger generation was so angry, while not suffering half what she and great-great-grandmother Tanner suffered. She would tell me, "Forgiveness, Larry. They haven't learned to forgive."
>
> So from my grandmother I learned not to be "angry." I learned not to demonize whites. I learned to forgive. All that came early in my life. The decision to follow my grandmother's admonition to "trust God" came several years later.[116]

His grandmother was one who had tasted that essence of Christianity. Thus, she knew what it meant to forgive, she knew that was the key.

## The Legacy of Resentment

We've been talking about the holy legacy of slave spirituality; but we must remember that, from slave times, we also have an unholy legacy of resentment. Resentment of blacks towards whites and of whites towards blacks. We Christians have the only way out of this vicious cycle—and that way is Jesus Christ.

In order to understand this legacy of resentment, let us go back again to slave times and look at the psychology of master and slave. As you will recall, the masters had an innate sense (of which they were usually not conscious) that their slaves, although in a socially inferior position, were actually morally superior to them. They sensed that the slaves were going to heaven, while they themselves were going to hell. That is why, as many accounts testify, on their deathbeds they desperately begged their slaves to forgive them.

The master, by owning another human being and whipping him as if he were a farm animal, is committing a sin. The society around him, however, condones the sin. Just as today, when many sins (like abortion and fornication) have become socially acceptable, so at that time the sin of slavery was socially acceptable. But the master senses that he's not right with God. He feels guilty, but he doesn't know where the guilt comes from. So he goes to the white minister, and the minister tells him, "You're doing just fine; everything is OK." But the master still feels that something is wrong. He cannot or will not identify what it is, because he doesn't even know his own soul, he doesn't know his essence. All he feels is that this unnamed sense of wrongness is somehow bound up with his slaves.

What is he going to do about it? Not recognizing his sin, he won't ask forgiveness of his slaves (that is, until he is about to die and he feels the jaws of hell yawning to receive him). Instead, what he will do is to whip them harder. Maybe then the guilt will go away, this socially acceptable act will become more acceptable, and the anger will be justified. This is a ploy of our fallen nature: to try to run from the guilt of a sin by doing it again and feeling the temporary relief of getting away with it.

The human ego by its very nature has to be on top of everything: over other people, and ultimately over God Himself. If it can't get above other people by power, authority, charisma, etc., then it will seek to get on top through resentment.

The slavemasters, of course, were on top to begin with. As they stood over their slaves and beat them, their egos felt an exhilaration of power. This, combined with the rage of unacknowledged resentment, made them feel, if only for a brief time, that in fact they were superior human beings to the slaves: not only socially but morally and spiritually as well.

In some cases, the masters openly betrayed their secret desire to play God by dominating the slaves. Former slave Daniel Dowdy recalls:

> They whipped you till you said, "Oh, pray, Master!" One day a man was saying, "Lord, have mercy!" They'd say, "Keep whipping that nigger, goddam him." He was whipped till he said, "Oh, pray, Master! I got enough." Then they said, "Let him up now, 'cause he's praying to the right man."[117]

Recently I wept in reading the story of a teenage girl in the times of slavery. Her master lusted after her, and when he wrongly suspected her of going to see another man, he called her to himself and accused her. She told him that she had only gone to get a bar of soap from the lady who lived next door. He said he didn't believe her, but she stuck to the story because it was the truth. So he took her outside, tied her to the ground, and had one of the other slaves whip her. As she was being whipped the girl was crying, "Master, have mercy! Master, have mercy! Oh, God! pity me." But the master ground his teeth, stamped the ground, and screamed at the slave to strike harder. This slave was a believing Christian man, and was going through inward turmoil. Finally he threw down the whip and declared that he could whip no more. The master threatened the slave with a severer flogging than the girl received if he refused to go on, but the slave, risking the consequences, would still not pick up the whip. Then the master took the whip up and beat the girl ten times harder than the slave had, until her back was absolutely ripped up. Blood was flowing down her sides, and finally she stopped screaming. The slave later recalled how the master was filled with a blind, insane rage at this totally innocent girl.[118]

We've talked about how Christian forgiveness is superhuman, divine. Well, the rage I've just described is also not human: it's subhuman, demonic. It's the lust of the ego to be on top of everything, through power and resentment. As that master was standing above the girl and whipping her, the more he did it the more he felt that it was OK. For that moment, he felt that he was somehow vindicating everything.

To bring this even closer to home: we do this every day when we judge and condemn other people. Through resentment, we think that we're on top; we feel a certain exhilaration, which seems to prove that we're really OK, we're not really sinners ourselves, because we're standing in judgment of the other person. We look at their sins so that we don't have to look at our own. Often we see the same sins in them that we have in ourselves, and we project the guilt onto them.

But this resentment, judgment and condemnation, while giving us temporary exhilaration, slowly eats us up inside. Mostly it hurts us, not the people we resent. For many of us, like the slavemasters, we have to be lying on our deathbed before the horrid reality of our condition catches up to us.

## Resentment Today

Having looked at the source of racial resentment in slave times, let us look more specifically at its legacy today.

From the point of view of the black man, the situation remains fairly simple. The blacks have endured and still endure injustices, and are tempted to respond with the resentment that destroys their souls. What's new about the current situation, however, is that black politicians and leaders are now, more than ever, trying to gain power by inculcating resentment and victim-psychology in black people. Rev. Jesse Lee Peterson, who is working to reverse this trend, writes:

> I grew up on a plantation near the small town of Midway, Alabama. My grandmother and grandfather worked this plantation all of their lives. They never owned the land they worked, and they were subject to the authority of the white owners. Yet, I never heard my grandparents speak with hateful attitudes about them. Frequently, I would hear them speaking of other problems, but they never blamed whites for their problem or their condition. I realize that they had just cause to disagree with their situation and also reason to blame. But as far as I can tell, they never did. We were close as a family. We had respect for adults and for one another. We went to church on Sunday and not once did I ever hear a [black] preacher who taught hatred or who blamed the white man. The focus of the preachers' message was always love and forgiveness. The neighbors knew each other and the children of each family, and so did the teachers.
>
> Today, thirty to forty years later, the black family has been nearly destroyed. Public schools are no longer about academics but mostly concern themselves with issues such as homosexuality, abortion, ways to have premarital sex, and other destructive ideas—a clear example of the forbidden fruit. There are more babies born out of wedlock

than ever before in history. Bastard children are no longer an embarrassment. The father, the originally intended and designated head of the family, has been relegated to a lesser role and stature than the mother, and in many television shows the father is ridiculed.

Rather than addressing these issues as their top priorities, the so-called civil rights leaders such as Congresswoman Maxine Waters, the Reverend Jesse Jackson, Louis Farrakhan, and Al Sharpton seem to be set on brainwashing the black community through a constant fomenting of discord and hatred towards the white man. . . .

Dr. Martin Luther King urged blacks not to hate anyone or anybody. Whenever you hate, it is impossible to see or know the truth. Dr. King knew that with hatred in the hearts of black people, they would not be able to see the Promised Land. It seems to me that if these "leaders" cared about the black people, they would put their time and energy into trying to determine the cause and effects of the drug use and how to effectively stop or remedy the situation.

Both black and white liberals have cleverly learned the art of mind control, and over the past 30 to 40 years they have continued to repeat the idea that the United States and the white man are the enemy. As with any lie, once you believe it, you can no longer be controlled by the truth, but by the lie, and controlled by the persons who tell the lie. This is quite clear in the black community. Most blacks are so asleep to the truth that they will not question the people who tell them that they cannot make it; that they must have programs such as affirmative action, welfare, and other governmental programs. Jesse Jackson, Louis Farrakhan and their wives and children are not on these programs. Their children have both mother and father in the home. They live in very good neighborhoods and the children attend the best schools. If whites are holding blacks back, why haven't these leaders and their families been held back? . . .

I was a victim of these people once. I believed white people were the total cause of my problems. I was nearly destroyed as a result of believing the lie. That is why I fight.

I hope this article will be instrumental in helping people of all races to wake up, and begin to think for themselves. I also want people to become aware and alert to the brainwashing techniques of these "leaders" and others like them. We must take full responsibility for our own lives. That is so wholesome. So healthy. So, I believe, pleasing to our Creator.

Fathers and mothers should take back their children from the influence of these "leaders" by teaching and showing them the right way to deal with life. They should show their children how to recognize good and bad in people of all colors and/or races; teach their children how to forgive the injustice of their enemies and themselves.[119]

When I spoke recently with Rev. Peterson, he told me that the above-mentioned leaders are deliberately instilling resentment in black people in order to hold them down, knowing full well that resentment debilitates the human being. This is because, if black people are held down and debilitated, they will be dependent on the corrupters who have done this to them. They will give them their votes, support and undying allegiance.

Likewise, the white leaders and officials who give out welfare are corrupting and debilitating those who are wrongly dependent on it. In the case of both the black and white false leaders, Peterson says, "the motive is simply wealth and power."

Because of his plainspokenness, Rev. Peterson has been attacked and reviled from all sides. When I asked how he himself is able to forego resentment and to forgive, he said, "It's so easy to forgive. When people attack me, I know that it's not them that is attacking, but the demonic spirit of anger working through them. I don't take it personally, but stand there and observe it, and it's as if it's happening to someone else. I have God, so I don't need to preserve myself. And I know that people filled with anger are hurting themselves, not me. They only hurt me when I begin to resent it. *Then* they've got me. That's what they want, in order to gain control over me. But I don't give in. I forgive them."

This response to injustice is precisely what was experienced by catacomb Christians throughout history, all of whom perceived that their enemies were destroying their own souls, and thus they prayed for them. They did not shy away from torture and death; they only shied away from hatred; for they knew that hatred, not torture, could destroy their souls and separate them eternally from God.

## Resentment as the Mark of Anti-Christ

From the point of view of the white man, the legacy of resentment is, on one level, not too different from what it was in slave times. There is still the racial prejudice arising from total ignorance of the human nature common to all of us. There is still the fallen human need to find an external scapegoat for one's internal sins, to blame those who look different so as not to have to face the real guilt in oneself.

In the last thirty years or so, however, there has grown up a new source of resentment in whites. In many places, as Rev. Peterson points out, whites are resentful of the special treatment and special opportunities given to blacks. "It's like a child hating a sibling for getting special treatment by his parents," says Rev. Peterson.

Such is the vicious cycle of resentment: resentment building upon resentment. Where will it end? In this country, it seems, it will end in a race war which will undermine the fabric of our society, making it necessary for a supreme "problem-solver" to come in and set things in order. Ultimately, this will usher in the anti-Christ.

Nearly two centuries ago—in the year 1813—Monk Theophan of Mount Athos, Greece, recorded the posthumous prophecies of St. Nilus the Myrrh-gusher, who revealed to him that the spirit of the anti-Christ in the last times will be precisely the spirit of resentment:

> Resentment is the mark of anti-Christ, and the heart of a spiteful person is sealed with this mark. When anti-Christ (the spirit of anti-Christ acting in the world) places this seal, then by this mark of resentment the heart of man becomes faint. It becomes as if dead, incapable of grief for sin, fear of God, or any other spiritual feelings. The Saint [Nilus] disclosed the root of the main disturbances of mankind as revolutions, hatred of children for parents, and other discords. These discords are all caused by resentment, or the prideful censure of the shortcomings of our neighbor, disrespect for parents, insubordination to authority, etc. If we consider the spirit of the times and the manner of activities of the enemies of the Church and state, we shall see that they base their whole success chiefly on this, in order to poison people by censure and hatred, and having infected them, to make them their obedient instruments.[120]

## Breaking Out of the Cycle of Resentment

As this prophecy indicates, the mark of resentment on the human soul begins in childhood, often with hatred for parents. The child learns to falsely gain mastery over injustices by resenting his family members or peers who have hurt him. This resentment can be either buried or open, but in any case it becomes an unconscious habit of the soul. Later, when the child grows up, he habitually finds other outlets wherein he can feel the exhilaration and false mastery of resentment: in racial hatred, bitterness toward authority, etc.

Thus, in dealing with racial hatred, it is often necessary to begin by facing one's childhood resentments. Rev. Jesse Lee Peterson told me that when he realized his unacknowledged resentment towards his parents and fully forgave them—at that moment he ceased to have racial hatred. He broke the habit of resentment and took up the habit of forgiveness.

The only way out of the cycle of resentment is the miracle of

Christian forgiveness, as experienced by the Catacomb Church in ancient times, by Christians under totalitarian regimes in our own century, and by the slave confessors of America.

If, as St. Nilus prophesied, resentment will be the mark of the anti-Christ, then divine forgiveness, as experienced by the catacomb slave Christians, is the seal of Jesus Christ in our souls. And if, as St. Ignatius says, people who do not know the Kingdom of God within them will take the anti-Christ's mark of resentment, then we must come to know that Kingdom by ceasing to resent.

## The Unique Position of Orthodoxy Today

The only way out is Jesus Christ, by whom we are changed from the inside out, by whom we are saved. That's why we Christians have a unique opportunity for witness in these times of growing resentment on all sides.

Also, as *Orthodox* Christians we are in a unique position to show to the world the real spiritual dimension of the African-American slave experience. We have this first of all because ancient Orthodoxy, more than any other expression of Christianity, has preserved an understanding of redemptive suffering; and secondly, because Orthodoxy knows the value of remembering one's ancestors and drawing strength from their witness.

At our 1996 meeting, I expressed the wish to find records of some slave martyrs, and we did find them. Now I have another wish. That we Orthodox Christians would come out with books bearing testimony to what went on, spiritually speaking, during slave times. A book for our young children so that they will be formed by images of these heroes; a book for young teenagers so that they will continue to grow up with these images; and then a book for adults which will present what we've been discussing in these conferences.

Such books could begin to lift the veil of worldliness that lies over our society at large, obscuring the otherworldly reality of black American history. Their purpose would be not only to show the truth of what happened, but more importantly to show its meaning for us today, as we approach the times of the anti-Christ, whose mark is resentment.

Our society is now changing spiritually at a rapid pace. Even secular commentators on the world speak of a "quickening" process. It could very well be that during our lifetime we will experience, in some form, the suffering and persecution that has been and still is experienced by the catacomb Christians throughout the world. The twentieth-century Orthodox prophet, Elder Ignatius of Harbin, has warned us, "What began in Russia will end in America." Already we see a steady deprivation of religious freedoms. There are people in high places who would like to see all our freedoms removed. Through the power of resentment they will try to bring us to such a state where it will seem necessary for them to come in and "take care of us." That is why we must respond with the power of forgiveness and the indomitability of Christian humility, through which we shall not be shaken.

To help prepare ourselves for times of suffering, want and religious persecution, we have examples and models of people who already have gone through this on our own soil: the righteous slave confessors. How did they get through it, and how can we do likewise? Their witness is especially meaningful for black Americans, but as I said earlier, it should be meaningful for all Americans who thirst for righteousness. In a time of superficial Christianity and religious fakery everywhere, they show us the way to elemental Christianity, which can lead Americans to the fullness of historic Christian experience in Orthodoxy.

Let us pray for them, and let us ask their prayers for us, that we truly enter into the essence of Christ's teaching as they did, and attain the Kingdom of Heaven with them. Amen.

# III
# TESTIMONIES

# 9

# HOLY
# UNMERCENARY
# HEALERS

## CARLA NEWBERN THOMAS, M.D.

HOLY UNMERCENARY HEALERS are servants of Christ, the focus of whose ministry is healing. The word "holy" comes from the Old English *haelig,* meaning "sacred," set apart for God. "Unmercenary" is derived from the Latin root word *merced,* meaning "reward." "*Un*" means "no." An unmercenary serves with no expectation of material reward, whereas a mercenary is well paid. The word "healer" comes from the Old English root word *haelen,* meaning "to make whole or restore." In comparison to modern physicians, holy unmercenary healers seek restoration of the body, mind and soul.

The goal of healing is to bring glory unto God, through reestablishing wholeness in Christ. To be complete, healing must occur in the three spheres of body, mind and soul. Seeking healing only of the body is like using a Band-Aid to bind a wound that is three inches deep. It won't work. While a whole body that is healthy is a blessing, it seems to be true that, as St. Paul and the beloved sufferer Macaria[121] demonstrate, some virtues of the soul cannot be obtained without a thorn of the flesh.

An unmercenary is full of mercy, pity and compassion. To have mercy towards someone means, in essence, to reward him with your compassion. The Apostle Paul calls us to "as the elect of God, holy and beloved, put on tender mercies, kindness, humility, meekness, long-suffering. . . ." (Col. 3:12) Healing has an appointed role in the Church. In I Cor. 12:28, Paul enumerates: "God has appointed these in the Church: first apostles, second prophets, third teachers, after that miracles, then gifts of healing, helps, administrations. . . ." It is an apostolic work, as we see in Matthew 10:8, where the Lord exhorts His disciples to "heal the sick, cleanse the lepers, raise the dead, cast out demons. Freely you have received, freely give." Unmercenaries are healers who give freely, receiving in return heavenly joy rather than worldly goods. We are all called to reject the spirit of greed, in favor of the spirit of charity and mercy—to be in a real way, unmercenary.

## A Treasury of Unmercenary Healers

The quintessential unmercenary is Jesus Christ. Christ elucidates the healing focus of His ministry by using Isaiah's prophecy in Luke 4:18, "The Spirit of the Lord is upon Me, because He hath anointed Me to preach the Gospel to the poor; He hath sent Me to heal the brokenhearted, to preach deliverance to the captives, and recovering of sight to the blind, to set at liberty them that are bruised." In his footsteps follow a golden army of saints who were extraordinary healers.

There are three distinct sets of Saints Cosmas and Damian who were unmercenaries. The first two were from Asia Minor. The second were murdered by their teacher while collecting herbs—they were from Rome. The third set of unmercenaries named Cosmas and Damian were from Arabia. After refusing to take part in pagan sacrifice, they were tortured. Stones flung at them boomeranged back to strike the throwers. Eventually, they were beheaded under orders from Lysias, the governor. I have opened a bookstore named "Saints Cosmas and Damian," to introduce people to Orthodoxy, to the fullness of Christ and his Saints. Appropriately, it also specializes in medicinal herbs.

The feast day of Great Martyr Panteleimon is July 27. Born of Eubula, a Christian, and Eustorgius, a pagan, St. Panteleimon received a solid medical education. After St. Hermolaus baptized him, he healed not only with medical knowledge but also through the power of Christ. His icon depicts a collection of medicinal ointments. When he was beheaded for being a Christian in 304, the olive tree, which stood over him, blossomed with healing fruit. The use of herbs and the appearance of the healing fruit show the role of earthly substance in the course of treatment of the heavenly soul. Panteleimon means "all merciful." He is my patron saint.

The life of St. Peter the Publican depicts another aspect of mercy. He was known as one of the stingiest men in Egypt. Once he threw a loaf of bread at a beggar in disgust. Later, in a near-death experience, he saw to his horror that this loaf was all that the angels had to tip the scales in his favor at his final judgment. Thus he learned the purpose of charity. Another unmercenary, Fabiola, was a physician who opened the first charity hospital in Rome. St. Jerome described her as "the mother of the poor and the consolation of the saints. . . . [I]f I had a 100 tongues and a 100 mouths and iron lungs, I should not be able to enumerate all the maladies to which Fabiola gave the most prodigal care and tenderness."

The Church commemorates Saints Cyrus and John on January 31. Cyrus (Kyros) was born in the third century in Alexandria, Egypt. Remembering that "of the Most High cometh healing," he healed by using medicine and calling on Christ. When a plan to assassinate him was uncovered, he fled to Arabia to carry on his work. There he met John, also a physician. Both were tonsured monks. They were known as *anargyroi,* meaning "unmercenaries." They returned to Alexandria to obtain the crown of martyrdom for Christ. The monk physicians dared to approach the magistrate Syrianos, seeking mitigation for the punishment of Athanasia, an imprisoned Christian woman. Their request denied, they were demonically tortured and executed. Their relics can be found at Abu-kir (Abba Kyros), Egypt.

On February 1, an unmercenary shepherd named Tryphon is remembered. When he was 17, he was given the gift of healing. The Emperor Gordianus summoned him from Phrygia (Central Turkey) to Rome because his daughter lay dying. After vigil and prayer, she was healed through Tryphon's efforts, calling upon the power of Christ. Rewarded with honor and gifts, Tryphon distributed his possessions to the poor and returned to the ascetic life of shepherding. He was martyred, under a different emperor, in 251 A.D.

Holy oil from the sepulcher of St. John the Wonderworker (a modern-day saint, who reposed in 1966) yields healing, too. My energetic son fell off of a bed when he was six years old and dislocated his right shoulder, leaving him in great pain. I tried to move the joint but it would not budge. Orthopedic surgery was the next step; the anesthesiologist had already been called. We decided to get one more x-ray. While my son was on the x-ray table for the last time before surgery, I remembered to anoint his shoulder with holy oil from St. John, and I prayed to Christ for healing, and to this beloved saint of latter times. The shoulder then slipped back into place, and surgery was averted. Glory be to God.

I believe that Dr. Martin Luther King can be considered a social unmercenary healer, for he sought to heal social illness. By embracing the Christian principle of obedience to God rather than man, he began a healing work on the American nation, riddled by the wounds of racism and hypocrisy. How can a nation proclaim liberty and justice for all when "injustice anywhere is a threat to justice everywhere"? Dr. King maintained, "Our aim must never be to defeat or humiliate the white man but to win his friendship and understanding."

## The Struggle to Be a Modern Unmercenary

As a family practitioner in Anniston, Alabama, I have tried, through God's grace, to follow in the footsteps of these holy unmercenaries. The following are instances in which I have put the principles of unmercenariness into practice.

A woman who had already been seen by a physician and nurse was admitted to me because it was my turn to take "med on call." Her work-up had already been done by the time I saw her. Still, I felt the need to talk to her. She was senile, but all people have a story to tell. As I listened, she began to talk aimlessly, but then whispered, "You know, I have a *special place*." I thought she was talking about Heaven, as the elderly speak of it frequently. Good-humoredly, I asked where this "special place" was. She went on to tell me about how she treats her special place with herbs like yellow root. To my horror, she then revealed a lime-sized breast mass with purulent drainage. She had metastatic breast cancer and is now receiving treatment. Listening is a healing art.

Unmercenaries must suffer and carry their crosses with courage. I was chastised for advice I gave a college student. She had a genitourinary infection. After securing treatment, I reminded her that sex is the gift of marriage, and abstinence is the rule before marriage. "When these laws are broken," I said, "you are at risk for contracting sexually transmitted diseases. Some of these diseases are curable by medicine, some are not." She reported to the dean that I had interrogated her unjustly. Despite this experience, I am unswayed in my mission. I try to counsel with compassion and without judgment, but sometimes there is no relief for the pain of the truth. Because I am called to speak the truth of God, I will not, to the dismay of many mothers and daughters, prescribe birth control pills for unmarried women for the prevention of pregnancy. Truly, one becomes stained with the sin by making a way for the sin to occur. This is a hard saying, even for those who work with me in my office.

A mother once sent her 15-year-old daughter alone to see me at a certain military installation about an abortion. I never mentioned the word "abortion," but counseled her about how actions have consequences, about the need for taking care of her body because of the new life within her, and about the fact that we all fall short of the Glory of God. "Though He is stern," I told her, "God is loving." The girl's mother had me written up and I was criticized by the Chief Medical Officer. After he finished his evaluation, I asked him one question. "What kind of mother sends her 15-year-old daughter alone to obtain major surgery?" He closed the case but destroyed my position there. I was paid according to the number of patients I treated, and over the next few weeks my clinics were progressively smaller. When only two people a day were scheduled for me, I finally saw the writing on the wall. Because of my contract, I could not be fired for unjust cause, but it was obvious that my services were no longer desired. Having lost 50% of my income, I resigned.

While working for an exclusive weight loss center, I encountered a prominent local businesswoman who declared she would not join the program if a black physician had to examine her. After consideration, I told the director (Caucasian) that I'd resign if she allowed the woman to join without a physical exam by me. The director, after her own deliberations, informed the woman that she would have to be examined by me. The client relented and I then examined her uneventfully. The director risked reputation and loss of income in order to do what was right before God. We have to remember that Moses tried peaceful means before resorting to parting the Red Sea. Too often, people resort to violent reaction first before trying the peaceful response. Mending the bridge is preferable to burning it, which was the temptation in this instance.

To maintain office peace, I have found that prayer is essential. I have an office that looks like a cross-section of America—all kinds of folks. We try to do staff prayers before meetings. Omitting them brings hellish havoc. In order to "spread the Gospel to the ends of the earth," I have icons on the walls and Christian magazines on the tables. My bookstore is there also. I also have a Bible-study ministry in two local prisons and a prayer group at the jail.

To care for prisoners, unceasing mental prayer is a must. To confront the spirit of greed and the false comfort of income in myself, charitable prayer is a must. Tithing 10% of one's income is a guarantee of blessing, to which I can testify. The first time I tithed this much, I received a letter three days later from a prominent insurance company rewarding me with a large sum of money for being a part of their company. This made no earthly sense to me. Managed care just doesn't work this way! I base my employee salaries as a percentage of my income and not just a set limit. This is actually an ancient Jewish custom to prevent extremes of wealth and poverty.

To battle the "doctor pedestal" mentality, humble prayer is a must. This last difficulty is the hardest. I remind myself that above all else, I am nothing. I am the daughter of a dentist, the daughter and granddaughter of teachers. I am the niece to aunts who taught Aretha Franklin and Della Reese how to sing in church. I am the granddaughter of a minister. My grandfather Daniel put 10 kids through college. Then, at the age of 72, he finished high school. My ancestors laid the foundation for me through their suffering, sacrifice and sense of duty.

I knew from an early age that I had the capacity to be a doctor. I attended Harvard Medical School, where I rose to meet the challenge of medicine but failed to learn the method by which the soul needed to be healed. Conventional medicine is woefully insufficient in its approach to the ailing soul. We have regressed. In antiquity, the priest and physician were one. Now we are separate and certainly not equal. Orthodox Christianity provides the missing link in the healing chain. "What profits a man if he gains the whole world and loses his soul," Jesus says. (Mt. 16:26) Similarly, what profits a man if he gains physical health but loses his soul? Nay, the three—body, mind and soul—cannot be effectively treated separately.

Most important is the planting deep within my soul the conviction that, of mine own self, I am nothing without the power of Christ. I choose to be Orthodox, to attain to the fullness of Christ in my being, while surrounded by others who shun the mysteries of God, including those who shun the Mother of God. Maintaining a humble spirit is one of the hardest things for me. No matter how a patient may look or talk, I remind myself that he is the image of God and that Christ is watching me! Unmercenaries heal by asking Jesus to heal. I find Christ, first. Then I focus my heart on Him by saying, "Lord Jesus Christ, Son of God, have mercy on him (the patient), a sinner, and open the doors of my heart. Mother of God, pray for him." Generally, I place my hands on the person's back and pray for healing of the body, mind and soul.

How often do we teach our children not to expect a material reward for every good deed? In this manner, we teach them to be unmercenary. We are all called to be unmercenary. To ward off the spirit of avarice, one must labor in the Spirit, knowing Christ works right along inside us.

I am married, with children, and have a significant mortgage. I employ eight people and have major financial responsibility. Yet, I seek the spirit of unmercenariness, the spirit of mercy. Several years ago, after consultation with a pastor, I started a special hour program. "Special hour days" are times when anyone can come to the office. I limited myself to two a day, and turned people away if I exceeded my quota. People were asked to pay whatever they could, even if this meant nothing. As God's abundance towards me has grown, I have stopped limiting the "free" slots. Now, I see everyone who comes through the door for clinic. The hollow feeling that I had at the beginning of my practice has lessened. I am learning the value of almsgiving, fasting and prayer.

Healing cannot be bought. Healing is something we can ask for, but always in the context of "Thy will be done." Let us seek healing like Shadrach, Meshach and Abednego, the three Hebrew children (cf. Daniel 3), who were willing to trust in God's providence for their deliverance from the fiery furnace. Let us enter into the crucible of life, looking for restoration of soul, rather than release from suffering. Let us carry our cross with joy. Let us be ready to suffer for redemption's sake. Let our dry bones and dry souls be filled with the Life-giving Spirit. Let us be adorned like the Virgin Mother Mary, with the beauty of holiness from our God and our Lord. Let us be restored by God's power through His only begotten Son, Christ the Savior. Like David, let the bones that are broken rejoice always in Jesus Christ the Lord.

# 10

## THAT THE GLORY
## OF GOD MAY BE
## MADE MANIFEST

### FATHER DEACON BISHOY COLE

I WANT TO SHARE WITH YOU how I came out of the darkness of the world into the light of Jesus Christ. I used to feel embarrassed to tell people about who I used to be and who I am, but then when I read the Scriptures I ran across a very deep chapter about the blind man. Christ was walking with His apostles when one of them asked Him, "What about this blind man? Who sinned, his father or his mother, that he was born blind?" And Christ looked at him and said: "Neither his father nor his mother sinned, but that the glory of God could be revealed in him." (Jn. 9:1-3) I often look at myself as that blind man because I'm here to give my testimony so that somebody out there can have hope. I believe this is why Christ sometimes allows some tribulation or problem in our lives—so that we can pull through it. Once we pull through and give honor to God, it helps the next person.

When I was a young man, a silly young man, a teenager 15-16 years old, I was the kind of person that would cause you to go and establish elaborate security systems around your house. I was the reason why you put your children in private school. I was a gang-banger on the streets of Los Angeles—drinking alcohol, smoking dope—crazy! I really thought I was cool, but deep inside I was scared to death. The only comfort I had was my homeboys. I remember standing on the street corners, ducking and running from

140

every car that I saw, thinking it was the police or one of my enemies trying to gun me down. You've all seen today's image of a gang-banger or a "crip" or a "blood"—people are scared to death of these individuals. Well, I was one of them.

It wasn't a "black" thing or a search for my roots. I wasn't searching for something. I was just scared. But the Lord gave me the spirit of repentance. He didn't "save" me, or pick me up and sweep me off my feet—there was a time I just decided that I was tired of this. At that time I didn't see any way out. If I had told my buddies, "You know I want to get out of this. It's not for me," they'd say, "You're going to get out of it alright, but you're going to get out of it in a casket." At the time, I really didn't think this solution was all that bad, because life didn't mean anything to me then. Taking a life didn't mean anything. Dealing crack didn't mean anything. But I was so fortunate that God delivered me by His Grace.

## A Change of Life

It began this way. One of my friends had a female cousin whom I really liked. One day she invited me to church. It was a Church of God in Christ. I went to that church the first night and people were jumping up and down. This was weird to me, emotional! But, I decided to keep on going and see if I could get this girl. I think that Christ was using this girl to see if He could get me. I didn't know what was happening. I was sitting in that church thinking that tonight we would go out together after church, and the preacher would be preaching, "Repent and be baptized and confess your sins." All this would go in one ear and out the other. She just kept holding that carrot out and coming to that church with me and then we could go somewhere afterward. This went on for the first week, the second week—and pretty soon it started to penetrate. She was up at the altar saying, "Thank you, Jesus!" and clapping her hands and I thought, "Okay, I guess I'll go up there too." So I went up to that altar, or platform, and I started clapping my hands saying, "Thank you, Jesus," just like everybody else. I'll tell you God's truth: I started getting these chills over and over and over. Pretty soon it became uncontrollable, so I just sat down and I started to cry, and I still do, to this day. Now I know why I'm crying, but then I didn't know. I had no idea why I was crying, but it seemed that through all these tears I shed I was releasing all of the sin and all of the wrong I had done in the way I was living. It was being released by all those tears.

I was probably 16 years old. After I dried my tears and got home

141

that night I was so sleepy and tired from everything that I just went to sleep. But when I woke up that next morning I was really changed. I don't know if it was the Holy Spirit. I wasn't baptized in water, but I had changed. I didn't want to be a crip anymore. I didn't want to gang bang. I still had the impulse to sin, but there was something imbedded in my mind now that told me when the impulse came that it was wrong, and it began to get stronger and stronger as each day passed. When I went out with one of my buddies to sit on the corner and drink some beer, I'd hear, "Wrong!" Somebody would give me a joint to smoke and I'd hear, "This is wrong!" It convicted me over and over again. That's why I marvel at the work of God and why I never judge other Christian religions. I could never say anything bad about the Church of God in Christ or any Protestant church or anybody in the Protestant church because I know that God is real and God works on anybody, anywhere, any church, any time He wants. He can even take you out of the Islamic mosque and change you into a Christian. I never doubt it.

## Back to the Gang

Well, as luck would have it, I got the girl. I said I was saved. I really was! There had truly been a transformation, a metamorphosis. I had been a gang-banger. Now I was a Christian. However, I started to be troubled in my relationship with that girl and eventually we broke up. Because I was so young, both physically and in the spirit, my relationship with that church also ended when we broke up. Needless to say, I went back to my buddies. We sat down, and started shooting the breeze as we always did. Instead of talking about the latest killing or who was going to get beat up next, I talked about the Bible. Nobody wanted to hear about the Bible. They said, "Man, you better cut that stuff out. You been in that church, going crazy!" I just kept talking about the Bible because it was in me.

Then I got myself into a real situation. I had about 15 buddies that I used to run with all the time and three of them were guys that I grew up with. We went to the same nursery school and the same junior high school and now we were in high school together. One of them was much older and in the first year of college. I'll never forget how one of my friends came up and said, "You know what? Mark Edwards just got shot." Mark Edwards was one of my closest friends. This was my opportunity to go to those brothers and prove that I was really one of them. He had been lying in his car and somebody shot him in his head over a drug deal. When you're in a gang, the only thing that goes through your mind in this kind of situation is revenge. We had to get revenge. That's how the cycle starts: violence and then revenge, and it just keeps going. That was the cycle that we were caught in. While everybody was packing up their guns and getting ready to get in the car and go take revenge, I just said to them, "Man, maybe we just need to let this one go and go and see Mark's mother." Right then and there I knew that they were against me. They looked at me with such hatred I thought they were going to turn their guns on me. They went and got their revenge and the one who did the killing of the other gang member is now doing life in prison. This is an example of how something very unfortunate can happen which can scare you. I had to realize that God is real and I could have been the one going to jail. These things were running through my mind.

At this time there was a rival gang at the school I was going to, and they identified me as one of the guys who helped kill their friend after one of their friends had killed our friend. By God's providence I managed to escape that situation. I remember being punched in the eye a couple of times and pushed around a few times, but I never went back and told my buddies because they weren't with me. I was a Christian now and they didn't want to hear about the Bible. Now I had my own buddies against me and I had this rival gang trying to get me. I was isolated. Do you know who my only friend was? The Lord! He was with me, but I didn't know it. I was just 16 years old. What was I going to do? I knew I had had this experience in my heart. All of this happened in a three- to six-month time span. It all hit me like a ton of bricks. I didn't know what was going on! Even after it was over there was nowhere I could go to give thanks because I had no church to attend. So I sat in my room and started to shed tears again. I was suffering. I probably cried more during that time than I ever cried in my life. I told myself that I would never tell anyone about these experiences, but it goes back to the blind man. If I can tell my story and somebody else can benefit from it, I've done my job. I will feel that I've done what God has put me here for, to glorify His Name through what He has done for me.

I was still a radical person, though. When you're a gang member you just hate everything and everybody. I was kind of racist. I blamed white people for a lot of things that my folks went through. My dad went through all that segregation—the Jim Crow laws, being called a nigger. As it says in Ezekiel, "The parents have eaten sour grapes and the children's teeth are set on edge." (Ez. 18:2)

## African Christianity

So here I was, searching again. Now I started wandering off from Christ and wanting to become a black militant. I wanted to resurrect the black man. So I went over to the house of this other black militant one day and said, "Tell me what you're about." Yet I still had this spark of the Holy Spirit in me, even though I didn't have a church. The spark was almost out. So I stepped in this person's living room. He had pictures of the Virgin Mary, Haile Selassie and the Patriarch of the Ethiopian Orthodox Church. I knew nothing about any of this. I saw a picture of this king with a crown and said, "What is this?" He told me that this was the emperor of Ethiopia. "What's Ethiopia? . . . Oh, okay, it's in Africa. Great! Tell me about Africa!" He said, "I'll tell you what happened. This was a line of 325 kings starting with King Menelik, who was the son of the Queen of Sheba and King Solomon." I couldn't believe it! King Solomon! From the Bible! Then he showed me this other picture of a patriarch with a staff and he told me that this was a patriarch, the head of the Ethiopian Church. At this point the light went on! "Church? An African Church? Tell me more about this." He took me to a Coptic Church. My friend thought he was just going to take me there and then we could go off to start rapping in poetry and get into this militant thing. But in my thoughts, he was taking me to Church, and that was what I needed.

I walked into the Coptic Church in Los Angeles and the first thing I noticed was that it smelled like I was in heaven. I had never smelled frankincense before in my life. Then I started to look around at all the icons. I saw the whole story of Christ in those icons, from His birth to His miracles, sitting on the throne, His Passion, Crucifixion, Resurrection and Ascension. I walked into that church and saw it all. I was young, but I was ready for anything. Then a man walked out from behind the veil. He was an Egyptian man from Alexandria. He really impressed me—he had a huge long beard, a little turban, a black robe and a big cross. I'd never seen anything like it in my life. Somehow I knew, that this was a *real* priest. I was used to seeing preachers in three-piece suits yelling and screaming behind the pulpit. That was all my exposure had been up to that point. I thought that the way to get the Word across was to scream and shout and have a band playing in the background. This priest asked me my name and showed so much love. I mentioned earlier that I was really bitter about race, about what my father had been through. This man who walked from behind the veil, was a white man (in my mind). I later found out that he was an African.

He sure looked white to me! But he showed me so much love, so much kindness that it was hard for me to hold some kind of racist feeling against people whom I really didn't know based on their skin color. He began to talk to me about who I was and what I went through. Of course, I wasn't telling him anything. I told him who my parents were and things like that. He invited me to have Bible study with him. We started meeting on Sunday nights. He didn't invite us to the Holy Eucharist for probably three or four months. So I began to come to Bible study with him and he began to tell me about Christianity. He didn't come right in and start telling me about the history of the tradition of the Orthodox Church. We just opened the Bible to Luke or Matthew and started talking about love and precepts on how to live a Christian life. My first lesson was a lesson on Galatians 5:15-22. I'll never forget this for as long as I live. He laid out for me the fruits of the spirit and the works of wrath, so clearly. For instance the ways of wrath are jealousy, hatred. Conversely, the fruits of the spirit are love, joy, and peace. At the level I was on, it gave me a clear understanding of what was right and what was wrong. More importantly, it told me the characteristics you need to possess to actually live in a correct way, as God would have us live. I wanted to bring somebody else to experience this. I figured that my buddies would not think this was corny, because it was not the kind of church like they were used to seeing. I figured that they'd look at this and say, "Wow!" So I called three of my best friends, who were in my gang: two Tony's and a guy named Ace. Now there were four of us and we continued our Bible study about four months. Finally, the priest asked us if we wanted to be baptized. I was wondering when he was going to ask me because I was ready to be baptized after my first conversation with him! It was about 1979, in the spring, that we were baptized. One of my friends was baptized Athanasius. Another was baptized Tekla Haimanot, and the other became Marcus. We all went back and tried to tell everybody that we had found this great church. But they wouldn't have it. They wouldn't have any of it. So, what can you do? If I reflect back even today . . . on Anthony who was another friend of mine who is a crack head now; or on Randall who is running around with a bullet lodged in his head and 35 years old, but still living in the same room he did then, I have to just thank God that He came into my life and turned me around.

## Church of the Apostles

I didn't find out until later why I'm here—I came to the ancient Christian Church because it is the only church that provides for me the foundation of a 2,000-year tradition dating from the time of Christ until today. It provides me with a ready reference for all the problems I have run into during my journey. When I have problems I pick up some words from St. Anthony about how to solve it. It's there, or in St. Augustine or the Desert Fathers. The Orthodox Church is like a treasure chest full of knowledge; it sustains me in my spiritual life every day. The Orthodox Church is a cycle. You keep up with all the facts and all the feasts; it'll keep you busy. It's not something you just go to every Sunday. It's not something you dress up for at Easter or Christmas so that you can go and listen to the preacher, give your offerings, have your crackers and grape juice and go. It's a whole lifestyle. I could have been Russian Orthodox. I could have been any kind of Orthodox because one common element in Orthodoxy is that *it is a life*. It has a circular life that you lead in the church. In fact, it sustains me. It is how I was able to come from where I was and be where I am today. As a gang member I very seldom went to school but one man turned me around. He put the idea into my mind that I needed an education. I did not know how to register, or what school to go to. I thank God that since that time I finished my high school, I also finished college, because of Christ. It just shows you that when God comes into your life, He just permeates all of you. He teaches you how to read. He teaches you how to write. But *you* have to do the work. You have to acknowledge that you want this and, if it's right and in God's plan, you go for it and you get it. God made us, not man. He did it. If the pope of any church decides to convert to Islam tomorrow, I'll still be Christian. No man can affect how Christ has come in and changed my life.

I'm a living example of how the power of God can come into somebody and change his life from bad to good. A lot of people have poured out God's love on me. Now, I can say that I don't have a racist bone in my body or any feeling of hatred for anybody. Because He wiped all that away. As a matter of fact, where I go to Church, I'm the only one of my kind—the only African-American— and I take this as a message from God. I guess I have the benefit of getting special treatment, but I don't mind. This has proven to me that everybody is not bad. I believe in my heart that the majority of people are good people. We make a mistake when we start stereo-typing. I love everybody through Christ. I think the Orthodox Church has been, and will continue to be, a sane factor in my life, because I feel in the depths of my heart that there's nowhere else for me to go. Once you've been Orthodox, there's nowhere else to go. I thank God that He brought me to the One Holy, Catholic, and

146

Apostolic Church. He chose to bring me here. I never like to criticize anybody's church because of my own conversion experience. I don't tell people that they are wrong to be Catholic or Protestant. What I tell them is that it's like this; you got a Volkswagen but I'm riding in a Mercedes Benz.

My mother likes to brag that she used to pray for me all the time. She used to always sit up waiting for me when I entered the house dressed up all crazy like a criminal. She would see me passing by and say to herself, "Lord, my boy's going astray." I used to always hear her say that. About two weeks before she died, my mother was baptized on her deathbed. My dad is pretty happy about how I turned out, though all he sees is the fact that I was able to finish school and get a good job and have a house, a wife and kids. I still try and tell him, "God did this!" He says, "Yeah, but you're doing a good job, son." My brothers, they're just holding on to their lives. They'll probably die in jail.

# 11

# MY JOURNEY TO ANCIENT CHRISTIANITY

## MARINA THOMPSON

JUST TO TELL YOU A LITTLE BIT ABOUT MYSELF, I was born in 1965 in San Bernardino, California. My father was in the Air Force, and we moved to Colorado Springs, Colorado when I was young and that is where I was raised. I have four brothers and two sisters. It was a large family. I remember that a man in a yellow school bus came by our house one day and asked my parents if they would send their children to church, and they said, "Gladly!" that they would, because there were seven of us. We all went. For many years I thought that they were just trying to get rid of us, but as I look at it now, I know that my father and my mother had actually given me to God through this.

Around the time I was in the third grade, I was baptized. The church was Christian and non-denominational. Every time the doors were open, I was there, because something had happened to me. That church became everything that I wanted. I loved the church world, and I never stopped going.

When I was fourteen years old my mother died of cancer. For me, that was the end of my life. It wasn't until two years ago, in my prayers to the Mother of God, that I stopped constantly grieving in my heart. My mother's death is no longer a pain that I walk around with. She died, and I had to reevaluate life, because I had always be-lieved that I would grow up, become a housewife, and have chil-

dren, and she would be there. I knew that she would be the grandmother of my children. My grandmother had died five years before
my mother and she was very important to me also. My world was
shaken and I had to reevaluate things. I decided at that point to fear
God. I reasoned, from a child's perspective, that if this God can take
away something as precious as a mother, without a cause, then I'd
better fear Him. I felt like I needed to do whatever He wanted. I was
making decisions for my life at fourteen. I decided then that I would
be a missionary, and serve God in whatever capacity He wanted
me to.

From high school on, I became a very serious person, very sober-
minded. I went to a Protestant Bible college in Manhattan, Kansas.
When I graduated, I felt I was still lacking something. From the time
I was in the eighth grade I always felt something was missing, something was missing. Even though, I was going to church constantly
and loving it, something *was* missing. Later I thought that it was the
Holy Spirit that was missing in my life. They didn't mention the
Holy Spirit in my church, except from time to time. When I entered
college, I visited every kind of church in the city. I didn't know
where to go. Nothing seemed to satisfy me. I was hungry for something more.

After graduating from college, I ended up moving to Kansas City
with a friend. I had to pay off a school loan. Although I had plans
and desires to be a missionary to Africa, I knew that I was neither
emotionally nor spiritually mature enough. When I came to Kansas
City, I said, "God, please do whatever to prepare me, because I want
to go." I began working to pay off my school loan, and ended up going to a charismatic church. During that same period I met David
and Thelma Altschul (now Fr. Paisius and Michaila). I didn't realize
it then, but it turned out to be at the planning meeting to form Reconciliation Ministries. It was in 1987. The following year, I started
going to church at Reconciliation Ministries.

I had been raised middle class, in the suburbs, with a totally different perspective of life and surroundings than that of the inner
city. Reconciliation Ministries was my introduction to it. I walked
through the door and heard the Gospel for the first time in my life,
even though I had been in a church since I was in the third grade. I
decided then that I wasn't leaving. I've been with David and Thelma
(Fr. Paisius and Michaila) in various ways now for years.

At Reconciliation Ministries, we went through a time when we
were doing a lot of outward service to the poor: helping the homeless, feeding people, visiting, and many other things. After several
years, we felt like we needed to reevaluate whether we were follow-

ing the proper path. We decided to shut down for a period of time to pray and to seek further direction. In that period of time we decided that we shouldn't open back up right away. At the same time, David and Thelma had started talking about different things out of the early Church. David had been teaching us for years about the early Church Fathers. He had been personally pursuing that path. I thought, I'm going to let them do their thing, and I'm going to just do my thing.

I ended up traveling with them, through California and up into Canada, for a couple of weddings. David, at that time, loved to stop at monasteries, so everywhere we were always looking for monasteries. We got to California, and went to a wedding. Then we started up the coast to San Francisco. David didn't know of any Orthodox monasteries beyond that, and so he began calling around. He had read a book, called *The Northern Thebaid*,[122] which was put out by the Saint Herman of Alaska Brotherhood. That stirred his heart, and he wondered at that time, "Does anybody live this way?" We didn't know this, but it was something that he was personally searching for. He began making phone calls while in San Francisco to find out if there was any place like St. Herman of Alaska Brotherhood. He wasn't expecting to find it, but in his phone calls they told him where it was, about three hours away. We immediately hopped in the car and drove like crazy to Platina, to the monastery. I remember going up the mountain wondering, "What are we doing?" At that time I wasn't really interested in beginning something else. I remember coming up the hill and seeing the monastery church, the dome through the trees, and thinking, "What in the world? Where are we?"

When we arrived, Father Gerasim, a monk, greeted us. He welcomed us and wanted us to stay. But the reality of what I was seeing didn't strike me until later.

The next day we left for Canada. Fr. Gerasim had given us a list of places to stay en route. He very emphatically told us right then, "You have to meet Father Moses [Berry] in St. Louis when you get back."

The night before, he had given us names of some people to meet in Portland, Oregon. We stayed in their home, and they told us about the Ethiopian Church. I thought, "Now *that* makes sense to me." I knew then that I wanted to become Orthodox. I didn't know how, and I really didn't personally even want to make the transition. But I knew. Just to hear about a people that had been preserved by God, and to know that they existed, was enough. In America, so much innocence and purity is robbed at such a young age. It's simply gone. To hear that people have been preserved by God was extremely important for me.

When we got back from our trip, we began praying the Orthodox prayers out of the Jordanville prayer book[123]—the morning and evening prayers. I remember saying to myself, "Even though these prayers are all about our sin, and confessing our sin to God, I say, 'Thank you,' because I know that Someone sees me." After all these years I can say that I am a sinner, and it's not a negative thing. It's not taboo to say that you are a sinner. To approach God in that way and to read those prayers was such a relief.

The prayers drew me in. One other thing happened during that period. We went to a women's conference in Indianapolis, at the St. Xenia Metochion. It was only the second Orthodox church that I had ever been in. The Metochion church is just a small chapel, on the third floor of their house. I remember going in there at night and weeping. I said, "God, you know, this is too much." All of the icons, the candles, the incense, the priests, everything—it was too much. I said, "Why this?" I remember at that time, we were venerating the icons (which I did not want to do). I went forward, because everybody else was doing it, and didn't want to just stand in the back. I went up before Jesus, and Jesus was standing in front of me.

It's just been like that in overcoming each obstacle that I've encountered in Orthodoxy. These were the very things that you were taught against in the Protestant world. Although these obstacles have been very difficult, God has helped me through them. I tell people now—my family and different people that I know that are not Orthodox—that I would not go elsewhere. This is it for me. I've found that Church that I sought for as a child, that I never wanted to leave.

# 12

## FINDING MY FATHERS: THE SEARCH FOR FAMILY IN AFRICAN CHRISTIANITY

### MICHAEL REDMOND

DRUGS WERE A PART OF MY LIFE—a major part of my life for a long time. I smoked my first joint at the age of nine. I hit the crack pipe, and had my last drink June 29, 1994. Glory to God, for the beginning and especially for the end! If it had not been for my addictions, I would not have known Jesus Christ, and I wouldn't be an Orthodox Christian.

I smoked weed off and on most of my life. Football was one of the things that helped slow the usage. I got pretty serious about athletics about age thirteen. It was the one thing that got me positive attention and the one thing that gave me some discipline. I was a very active young man until the age of eighteen. My drug usage was not as heavy then as it would become later. I wasn't one of the "bad" kids who stayed in trouble. Instead I was on the honor roll, a Lt. Col. in the Junior ROTC, as well as 1st Battalion commander over 162 cadets, and an above average athlete—great potential, with little guidance.

It was during high school that I met the love of my life, Linda Cheadle. She was the first girl who wouldn't give me the time of day. So, I proceeded to bug her until she gave in. We fell deeply in love—nothing or no one else really mattered. During my senior year of high school we had our first son, Steven Jr. Then the stress of being a man set in.

Before my son was born, I started working seven days a week, twelve hours a day at a security job. I also went to school four hours a day. It was during this same period that I was trying to decide where I wanted to attend college. I had my eye on UCLA to play football, even though my coach wanted me to get married. But I was too "full of myself" at the time. For although I loved Linda, I thought I was too young for marriage. She didn't want me to go away. I settled for a junior college in Highland, Kansas. I was pretty fortunate to have received an athletic and theater scholarship.

Shortly after starting college I came home on crutches. I couldn't play football, and without it there was no discipline. It was time to party. That demon that had haunted every man in my family came out now in full force. Every man in my family has at one time or another had an addiction to alcohol. My addiction became full blown. I went to college for only one more year. Life at home was different. Linda and Steve Jr. and I were living with my mother. We eventually got our first place—a roach haven. We ate fried potatoes for a week. I had begun drinking heavily and buying weed every week. Linda and I fought, and as is common among alcoholics and drug addicts, I was abusive.

One day my brother came over and together we smoked a joint that had rock cocaine in it. I was immediately hooked. The crash was hard and quick. Soon I began smoking out of a pipe, which was more intense. Eventually I ended up in jail, having stolen $645 from my mother to get high. She had me arrested. After I got there, a young man asked me if I was going to Bible study. I thought to myself, "This is jail! What is he talking about?" The young man continued to ask if I was going until it became irritating, and so I said "yes." I now recognize this young man as an angel of the Lord, because after I said I was going I never saw him again. I'm crying now as I remember this, because, in my darkest hour, when my mother had told me she didn't want to see me unless it was my funeral, and the woman I loved didn't need me, God chose me to receive the truth.

As I stepped into the room for the Bible study, I saw for the first time in my life a room full of black men in fellowship with God. I had been to church many times before, but that was the first time that I had ever seen black men, fifty or sixty of us, together in fellowship. I know many of you have experienced this—you walk into a room and a certain kind of fear—a knowing of the presence of God! I felt that. The next day I went back and decided to follow Christ. (This was Feb. 27, 1990.) The day after that I met David Altschul (Fr. Paisius). This was the first white man who made me feel totally at ease. He gave me a Bible and I was at his Bible study every time he came. One day he said that if any one doesn't want to go back to the situation or environment they came from, to let him know before they got out. Originally I was supposed to have 180 days in jail, but it was put on my heart to plead guilty. As a result, the judge let me out on probation and restitution. I was given early release.

There I was—downtown with no money, dirty clothes and a Bible. My first thought was to find a place to sleep, and a place to put down this Bible. After receiving $15 for a blood donation, I immediately went to the store, with my Bible in hand (only because I didn't have anywhere to put it). I bought some burritos and a 40-oz. bottle of beer. I stood at a pay phone outside the store, sat the Bible down under the phone, ate the burritos, popped the top on the beer and gulped about a fourth of it down. Immediately this feeling came over me—like never before. It was a fear, but different than terror. I dumped the rest of the beer out, and picked up the Bible. If anyone recalls a Gideon Bible, in the front it has a section that says, "For comfort, courage and strength," etc. Then it gives scriptures on these different topics. I began to turn to the scriptures for strength, when a gust of wind blew. It seemed to be quite strong enough to blow the Bible out of my hand. I caught it before it hit the ground. Before this I was concerned about where I would sleep—I had nowhere to go at all. When I grabbed the Bible I grabbed it by the front of the cover, and I saw the words "David Altschul, 3101 Troost" and the phone number. I tried calling him for about an hour, but he was not in. I then noticed that three 31st Street buses had passed me, and I heard a still soft voice from within say, "Get on the bus!" As soon as I reached the corner of 31st and Troost, David was parking his car. This caused me to remember the old saying, "He don't always come when you want Him, but He's always on time." Amen!

This was my beginning stage at Reconciliation Ministries. It was an inner city ministry made up of people from the inner city and suburbs, multi-racial, all trying to live out the life of Christ on earth. I then began to live off and on in what was simply known as the "Brothers House." I stayed there for the next three years. During this time I enjoyed a tremendous peace, with very little conflict. Much of my life had changed. There was no TV and only Christian music was allowed on the radio. There was prayer every morning at 6 AM. If you weren't working, you were to help out at the church.

I had lost Linda by this time, but the Lord showed me a great deal about myself. I battled jealousy for a very long time and,

through Christ Jesus, and no strength of my own, I was able to endure and begin to change. I had several jobs during this period and
eventually I left the Brothers' House. I went back to life with my
mother, Linda and Steven Jr. Gradually, I began to stay away from
church, and like a whirlwind, I relapsed in cocaine. Through benefits from my job, I was able to enter drug treatment. This experience
was good. It showed me more of myself. I was able to get back to
church for a while, and moved back to the House—everything
seemed fine. Linda and Steven lived at the church for a time and we
were eventually to be married, finally. Later the Brother's House
closed and once again I was on shaky ground. I started drinking. A
few months after this, I started buying weed, then I used cocaine
again. This was the worst time yet. I blew a lot of money in one
night.

I knew I had to return to treatment, and did. This was the first
time on my journey that I knew I couldn't make it without Jesus
Christ. After the first period of treatment, the fog lifted. I was able
to pray and I began to fast. After about a week I began to have
strong feelings and thoughts about Ethiopia, but I didn't know why.
I dreamed about men in black robes and funny hats. I knew nothing
of Orthodoxy at the time. Unfortunately, my going to treatment had
also ended my job. The Lord gave me comfort in this because I
knew it was wrong to be terminated for getting help for myself.
When I got out of treatment, I went home to a very abrupt reception. "It's over! I don't like you. I hate you. I don't want you around
any more." Through grace, I was led to the only refuge I've ever
truly known, at Reconciliation Ministries. I had a conversation
with Thelma, David's wife. She started telling me, "Ethiopia? Yeah,
look . . ." She proceeded to show me African icons and books about
African Christianity. Then I told her about the robes and she says,
"Well, yeah," and she gave me an earful of goodies. When I mentioned I had been thinking of Ethiopia, and dreaming about black
robes, her face lit up and she threw that big grin up and didn't stop
talking until I had to leave. I'm like, "Wow! That's heavy, you know."

I came back that next Sunday, but this time I came and I lived
right in the church, on the 4th floor. There had been a major
change since I had last been at the Ministry. At the time it was something I knew nothing about—Orthodoxy. All I knew was the black
robes and the word "Ethiopia" that I had in my dream. David (now
Fr. Paisius) and Thelma (now Michaila) and others had been apparently reading and studying about it, visiting monasteries and
churches, and had become Orthodox.

During this time when I was staying on the 4th floor, I prayed and hoped for healing for my family and myself. A priest from Ethiopia, Father Asteraye, came once and gave a talk. I had a chance to speak with him. He gave me a totally new light on a lot of things. He wanted me to try to get Linda to come and talk together. She didn't want to come at all, at first. She was pregnant, but she did come eventually. When Father Asteraye started describing the Orthodox view of life and marriage, he shed light on so many things. This was the way I had always felt about my children, especially my child Steven. He said simply, "A child is two parts, it is part of you, and it is part of your wife." He said, "If you do not have . . ." At this point Fr. Asteraye began to cry—I could feel him you know, it hurt him, that I didn't know my father, and my father didn't know me. This is something that I have always known, and yet I had never known it consciously. Father Asteraye said, "If a child does not have his father or his mother there is a part of him that does not develop."

So, I don't know if the Holy Spirit has raised that up in me, to be a father, or to fight and struggle, to want to love my children, but it's the desire of my heart. When I sit up and I look at my sons, I think, "I want to know them." You see, when I think of my father, I remember exactly what he looked like. I've met him twice, but I know exactly what he looks like. I'd know him if he walked in the door, and I look just like him. When I met him when I was sixteen, he didn't know who I was. Now, he doesn't know his grandsons, and I look like him, and they look like me. What Father Asteraye was saying hurts my heart—it aches. When I look at my sons, I see me. I look and I say, "He's got Linda's ears, and he's got my toes." All of this is miraculous to me, and nobody else has to understand this but me and God. I honestly know that's how it's supposed to be. The hard thing is that almost every black male I know in America has gone through this, or experienced what I've been through and what I feel. Yet, now, I'm not mad about it the way I used to be. I know I wouldn't be the man I am if I had not endured or went through all these things, but I know I've needed more.

One of the things that I have seen at the Conferences is black priests, black fathers. Although I have appreciated the love the white brothers and sisters have given me, for a black man to receive the faith from black fathers is very powerful. In this way, I have come into Orthodoxy. So many things have been answered for me—the blackness, my blackness, is finally being shown to me. Even though I always knew it was there, I never knew how it connected. Finally, somebody is not denying the fact that we exist, that we are part of God's family and purpose, and I needed that. When I come into the church, and I see the icons, I no longer see this white-skinned, blue-eyed Jesus that I grew up seeing. I don't know what He looked like, but I can't believe that he had blue eyes and blonde hair. I can't believe that, and that's all I've ever been taught. That's another factor that drew me into Orthodoxy—that's one of the things that sealed it for me. Then, to read about all the different saints and get the whole story and receive the tradition from the time of the Apostles, has been powerful!

Linda and I were finally married on Dec. 15, 1994. On the 21st of that month I got my job back. My second son, Benjamin, was born Jan. 31, 1995. Shortly thereafter, my family and I were baptized into the Orthodox Church. It was wonderful—the water was extremely cold. It reminded me of taking a cold shower when I was in my teen years when we didn't have any heat. But it was a wonderful experience, and I am so glad to be a part of it. I know this is my home. I know in my heart that this is where I am supposed to be. This is what will teach me the things that I don't know. This is something that my sons can see.

The other night I was at work. I called home, and Linda said, "Guess what?" I said, "What?" She said, "Guess who did the hours?" [i.e., reading from the daily cycle of Orthodox Prayers]. I said, "Who?" She said, "Steven!" [my son]. That's *very* important to me—from him seeing me do it, from him seeing his mother do it, the tradition, he's doing it.

Spiritual life is being passed on. From Jesus to the Apostles to the African Church to me and now to my sons. I have found the faith of my fathers. I have found the faith for my sons. May we all be given strength to keep it and the courage to pass it on to others.

# AFTERWORD
# FULL CIRCLE

# AFTERWORD

## ALBERT PANTELEIMON RABOTEAU

SEVERAL YEARS AGO, when I was considering becoming Orthodox, a friend and fellow historian of African-American religion asked me if I understood how much Orthodoxy fit the aspects of African-American religion that had most personally interested me over the years. Several months earlier an Orthodox monk had remarked to me how attuned he thought Orthodoxy was to the traditional spirituality of black people. Both comments took me by surprise. I had been so absorbed in the details of my own individual path toward Orthodoxy that I had failed to notice the forest for the trees, to discern the overall pattern my life was taking. Gradually after my chrismation, I began to reflect more generally upon the relationship between the faith of Ancient Christianity that had claimed me and the religious traditions of my people whose history I had been researching, writing, and teaching for the past twenty-five years. Since there are so few black Orthodox, it seemed like a lonely task. Providentially, a friend informed me of the conferences on Ancient Christianity and African-America out of which this book has grown. It was (and continues to be) the purpose of these conferences to gather people from around the country to discover in the context of prayer and the Divine Liturgy the deep affinities and resonances between Orthodoxy and African-American spirituality.

The resonances or points of convergence between Orthodoxy

161

and African-American spirituality, as my friend and the monk realized, are profound. The first resonance is historical. Ancient Christianity is not, as many think, a European religion. Christian communities were well established in Africa by the third and fourth centuries. In Egypt and Ethiopia, traditions of worship, monasticism, and spirituality have remained authentically African and authentically Christian down to the present day.

The second resonance is spiritual: there are analogies between African traditional religions and Orthodox Christianity. In classical theological terms these analogies constitute a protoevangelion: a preparation for the Gospel based on God's natural revelation to all peoples through nature and conscience. I would distinguish seven principal areas in which African spirituality *foreshadowed* ancient Christianity:

1. Traditionally, African spirituality has emphasized the close relationship, the "coinherence" of the other world and this world, the realm of the divine and the realm of the human. The French poet Paul Eluard expressed this insight concisely when he said, "There is another world, but it is within this one." Orthodoxy also emphasizes the reality and the closeness of the kingdom of God, following the words of Jesus, "The kingdom of God is within (or amongst) you." Indeed, the closeness of the heavenly dimension is graphically symbolized in Orthodox churches by the iconostasis, the screen which stands for the invisibility that keeps our visible eyes from perceiving the heavenly kingdom already present among us behind the royal doors. The icons hanging upon the iconostasis serve as so many windows upon this invisible, but ever present world, as do the lives of the saints that the icons represent. In both traditions ritual is understood to be the door that allows passage between the two worlds to take place.

2. Traditional African religions depicted the other world as the dwelling place of God and of a host of supernatural spirits (some of them ancestors) who mediated between the divine and the human and watched over the lives of men and women, offering, when asked, to protect people from harm or to provide favor on their behalf. Orthodox Christians believe in the power of saints, ancestors in the faith, to intercede with God for us and to protect and help us in time of distress.

3. African spirituality values the material world as enlivened with spirit and makes use of material objects that have been imbued with spiritual power. Orthodoxy sees the world as charged with the glory of God and celebrates in the feast of Theophany the renewal of the entire creation through God becoming flesh in the person of Jesus.

162

Orthodoxy also appreciates the holiness of blessed matter, and uses water, chrism, candles, icons, crosses, and incense in the celebration of the Divine Liturgy and the Holy Mysteries (Sacraments).

4. The person in traditional African spirituality is conceived not as an individualized self, but as a web of relationships. Interrelatedness with the community, past as well as present, constitutes the person. Orthodox theologians speak of the person as being radically interpersonal, a being in communion, ultimately reflecting the interpersonal nature of the Divine Trinity. And the corporate character of Christian identity is grounded in the reality of the Mystical Body of Christ.

5. African religions speak of human beings as the children of God, who carry within a spark of God or "chi," a bit of God's soul that animates the spirit of each man and woman. Orthodoxy, following Genesis, teaches that we are created in the image and likeness of God and that it is our basic vocation to be "divinized," becoming more and more like the image in which we are created.

6. African spirituality does not dichotomize body and spirit, but views the human being as embodied spirit and inspirited body, so that the whole person—body and spirit—is involved in the worship of God. Orthodoxy also recognizes the person as embodied spirit and stresses the importance of bodily gestures, such as signing the cross, bowing, and prostrating, in the act of private and public prayer.

7. The African-American spirituals placed a strong emphasis on a tone of sad joyfulness that reflected African-Americans' experience and their perspective on life. In Orthodoxy the sad joyfulness of the liturgical chant tones poignantly expresses the attitude of penthos or repentance which characterizes the Orthodox Christian's attitude toward life.

This tone of sad joyfulness relates directly to the third major area of analogy between African-American spirituality and Orthodoxy, the experience of suffering Christianity. Ancient Christianity prized the gift of martyrdom, the witness through suffering even death itself to the truth of the Christian gospel. Paradoxically Christians throughout history have seen periods of martyrdom, as periods of spiritual vitality and growth. "The blood of martyrs is the seed of the Church." Suffering Christianity, following in the pattern of Christ and the saints, has been for Orthodoxy a mark of the authenticity of faith. African-American Christians have offered a prime example of suffering Christianity in this nation and have understood their own tradition as an extension of the line of martyrs from the days of the ancient church.

163

# FULL CIRCLE:
# A FINAL WORD
# FROM THE
# BROTHERHOOD OF
# ST. MOSES THE BLACK

FR. MOSES BERRY

ANCIENT, APOSTOLIC, ORTHODOX CHRISTIANITY has gone full circle, from continent to continent, and back again. From Christ to His Apostles, from the Apostles to ancient Africa, from Africa to African-America, and from African-Americans to their sons and daughters. The ancient African Christian tradition *is* being passed on and taking root in America, growing out of the seed of the blood of black American slave-martyrs for Christ. Thanks to the Holy Spirit, nothing has been lost. The circle has now been completed. It is only ours to reunite ourselves with the unbroken circle of the Divinely inspired tradition.

Christ's Body, the Church, is also a circle. As this book has shown, not only are the people of Africa part of that circle, but they are a *key* part in the foundation and providential development of it. By founding the monastic tradition, they preserved the otherworldliness of true Christianity, setting the tone for the Church for the following 1,700 years, up until today. And then, even while cut off from the ancient line of African Christian tradition while suffering as slaves in America, they still—by a miracle of God—became a repository of otherworldly Christianity in this land.

Now that the link to the ancient African Christian tradition has been restored, the time has come to call black Americans back to the Unbroken Circle that is their heritage. This is our mission.

Our mission is not Afrocentric, for this would be to neglect the heritage of our righteous forefathers in America. Nor is it ethnocentric, for this would be to break the circle of the universal Body of Christ, which is composed of people of all nations and cultures. Rather, our mission is Christocentric. Christ is at the center of the circle. If we stay on the edge of the circle and try to draw closer only to those who look and act like us, we will of necessity draw farther away from all the rest of our brothers and sisters who are at different places on the circle. Therefore, we strive to draw closer to Christ at the center. When we all do this, then we at the same time draw closer to *everyone else*, not excluding anyone, which is the meaning of perfect love. We will meet at the center, in Christ, who is all, and in all.

Being Christocentric, we honor our forefathers not only because they were black, but because they were righteous black followers of our Lord Jesus Christ. The sweat and blood of their suffering for Christ and with Christ is our foundation, our seed, our root, our sustenance, our life-substance. We must find it, we must grow from it. Otherwise we will spiritually wither and die, as is happening in most of our American culture today—red, yellow, black and white— where people are cut off from their Christian roots.

The purpose of the Brotherhood of St. Moses the Black is *first of all*, to bring ancient Orthodox Christianity to African-Americans, and *secondly*, to root them and nourish them on the martyric experience of their righteous Christian forefathers and foremothers, both in Africa and in America. Again, this is not in order to create a separatist movement within Christ's original Church, but rather to provide the spiritual sustenance proper to people of African descent.

We strive to be at odds with the world in this sinful and adulterous generation, one in which the wisdom of the world has so obscured the Way, the Truth and the Life that all are in danger of being led into apostasy. This is a time when evil is everywhere proclaimed as good. In such a time, we cling to the Tradition of the Church as it has been preserved through the ages, so that we don't have to rely on our own understanding of the truth, tainted as it is by the spirit of this world. We know also that these are days in which, if we cling to this Holy Tradition, people will kill us and think they have done God a favor. (John 16:2) Nevertheless, we heed the words of St. Isaac of Syria:

> When you desire to pursue some beautiful work for the love of God, put death as the limit of your desire. In this way you will be deemed worthy to ascend in actual deed to the level of martyrdom in every

suffering and injury which you may encounter within this limit, provided that you patiently endure unto the end. . . . (*Ascetical Homilies,* Homily 62)

In this manner we go forth, trusting always in God and His saints.

Fr. Moses Berry, President
Brotherhood of St. Moses the Black

# APPENDIXES

# NOTES

# APPENDIX I

# AFRICAN-AMERICAN MARTYROLOGY

## I. Martyrs
## Those Killed for Praying

### 1. MARTYR EZEKIEL

"I have heard it said by people in authority, Tom Ashbie owned nine thousand acres of farm land besides wood land. He was a large slave owner, having more than a hundred slaves on his farm. They were awakened by blowing of the horn before sunrise by the overseer, started work at sunrise and worked all day to sundown, with no time to the cabin for dinner. You carried your dinner with you. The slaves were driven at top speed and whipped at the snap of a finger by the overseers. We had four overseers on the farm, all hired white men. I have seen men beaten until they dropped in their tracks; or knocked over by clubs; women stripped down to their waist and cowhided.

"I have heard it said that Tom Ashbie's father went to one of the cabins late at night. The slaves were having a secret prayer meeting. He heard one of the slaves ask God to change the heart of his master and deliver him from slavery so that he may enjoy freedom. Before the next day the man disappeared, no one ever seeing him again. . . . When old man Ashbie died, just before he died, he told

169

the white Baptist minister that he had killed Zeke for praying and that he was going to hell."

(From an interview with ex-slave Rev. Silas Jackson in Baltimore, Maryland. Age when interviewed: 90. Federal Writers Project, 1936-1938.)

## 2. MARTYR MARTIN (CHARLOTTE MARTIN'S BROTHER)

Charlotte Mitchell Martin, one of twenty children, was a slave of Judge Wilkerson on a large plantation in Sixteen, Florida, a little town near Madison. Shepherd Mitchell was a wagoner who hauled whiskey from Newport News, Virginia for his owner. Wilkerson was very cruel and held them in constant fear of him. He would not permit them to hold religious meetings or any other kinds of meetings, but they frequently met in secret to conduct religious services. When they were caught, the "instigators," known or suspected, were severely flogged. Charlotte recalls how her oldest brother was whipped to death for taking part in one of the religious ceremonies. This cruel act halted the secret religious services.

(From an interview with Charlotte Martin conducted by the Federal Writers Project in Live Oak, Florida, August 20, 1936.)

## II. Confessors
## A. Those Beaten or Imprisoned for Praying

### 3. SYLVIA AVERY

Mrs. Celestia Avery, an ex-slave, is a small mulatto woman about five feet in height. She has a remarkably clear memory in view of the fact that she is about 75 years of age. Before the interview began she reminded the writer that the facts to be related were either told to her by her grandmother, Sylvia Heard, or were facts which she remembered herself.

Mrs. Avery was born 75 years ago in Troupe County, LaGrange, GA, the eighth oldest child of Lenore and Silas Heard. There were 10 other children besides herself. She and her family were owned by Mr. and Mrs. Peter Heard. In those days the slaves carried the surname of their master; this accounted for all slaves having the same name whether they were kin or not.

The owner Mr. Heard had a plantation of about 500 acres and was considered wealthy by all who knew him. Mrs. Avery was unable to give the exact number of slaves on the plantation, but knew he owned a large number.

Mr. Heard was a very mean master and was not liked by any one of his slaves. Secretly each one hated him. He whipped unmercifully and in most cases unnecessarily. However, he sometimes found it hard to subdue some slaves who happened to have very high tempers. In the event this was the case he would set a pack of hounds on him. Mrs. Avery related to the writer the story told to her of Mr. Heard's cruelty by her grandmother. The facts were as follows:

"Every morning my grandmother would pray, and old man Heard despised to hear any one pray, saying they were only doing so that they might become free niggers. Just as sure as the sun would rise, she would get a whipping; but this did not stop her prayers every morning before day.

"This particular time grandmother Sylvia was in the 'family way' and that morning she began to pray as usual. The master heard her and became so angry he came to her cabin and seized and pulled her clothes from her body and tied her to a young sapling. He whipped her so brutally that her body was raw all over. When darkness fell her husband cut her down from the tree, during the day he was afraid to go near her. Rather than go back to the cabin she crawled on her knees to the woods and her husband brought grease for her to grease her raw body. For two weeks the master hunted but could not find her; however, when he finally did, she had given birth to twins. The only thing that saved her was the fact that she was a mid-wife and always carried a small penknife which she used to cut the navel cord of the babies. After doing this she tore her petticoat into two pieces and wrapped each baby."

Grandmother Sylvia lived to be 115 years old.

Not only was Mr. Heard cruel but it seemed that every one he hired in the capacity of overseer was just as cruel. For instance, Mrs. Avery's grandmother Sylvia was told to take her clothes off when she reached the end of a row. She was to be whipped because she had not completed the required amount of hoeing for the day. Grandmother continued hoeing until she came to a fence; as the overseer reached out to grab her she snatched a fence railing and broke it across his arms. On another occasion grandmother Sylvia ran all the way to town to tell the master that an overseer was beating her husband to death. The master immediately jumped on his horse and started for home and reaching the plantation he ordered the overseer to stop whipping the old man. Mrs. Avery received one whipping, with a hair brush, for disobedience. This was given to her by the mistress.

Slaves were given separate churches, but the minister who conducted the services was white. Very seldom did the text vary from the usual one of obedience to the master and mistress, and the necessity for good behavior. Every one was required to attend church, however. The only self expression they could indulge in without conflict with the master was that of singing. Anyone heard praying was given a good whipping; for most masters thought their praying not good since freedom was the uppermost thought in everyone's head.

(From an interview with Celestia Avery, conducted in Georgia by the Federal Writers Project in 1937.)

## 4. CANDUS RICHARDSON'S HUSBAND

Mrs. Candus Richardson, of 2710 Boulevard Place, was 18 years of age when the Civil War was over. She was born a slave on Jim Scott's plantation on the "Homer Chitter River" in Franklin County, Mississippi. Scott was the heir of "Old Jake Scott." "Old Jim Scott" had about fifty slaves who raised crops, cotton, tobacco, and hogs. Candus cooked for Scott and his wife, Miss Elizabeth. They were both cruel according to Mrs. Richardson. She said that at one time her Master struck her over the head with the butt of a cowhide, that made a hole in her head, the scar of which she still carries. He struck her down because he caught her giving a hungry slave something to eat at the back door of the "big house." The "big house" was Scott's house.

Scott beat her husband a lot of times because he caught him praying. But "beatings didn't stop my husband from praying. He just kept on praying. He'd steal off to the woods and pray, but he prayed so loud that anybody close around could hear, because he had such a loud voice. I prayed too, but I always prayed to myself." One time Jim Scott beat her husband "so unmerciful for praying that his shirt was as red from blood stain as if you'd paint it with a brush." Her husband was very religious, and she claimed that it was his prayers and "a whole lot of other slaves that cause you young folks to be free today."

They didn't have any Bible on the Scott plantation she said, for it meant "a beating or a killing if you'd be caught with one. But there were a lot of good slaves and they knew how to pray and some of the white folks loved to hear them pray too, 'cause there was no put-on about it. That's why we folks know how to sing and pray, 'cause we have gone through so much, but the Lord is with us, the Lord's with us, He is. . . ."

Mrs. Richardson says that she is "so happy to know that I have lived to see the day when you young people can serve God without slipping around to serve Him like we old folks had to do. You see that pencil that you have in your hand there, why, that would cost me my life if old Mas' Jim would see me with a pencil in my hand. But I lived to see both him and Miss Elizabeth die a hard death. They both hated to die, although they belonged to a church. Thank God for His mercy! Thank God! My mother prayed for me and I am praying for you young folks."

Mrs. Richardson, despite her 90 years of age, can walk a distance of a mile and half to her church.

(From an interview with Candus Richardson, conducted by the Federal Writers Project. Submitted in Indianapolis, Indiana, on August 31, 1937.)

### 5. REV. ANDREW BRYAN

Rev. Andrew Bryan was one of the first African-American Confessors of Christ. The following account of his life has been taken from *Slave Religion* by Albert J. Raboteau, p. 141:

George Liele, before he sailed for Jamaica in 1782, had converted a slave named Andrew Bryan (by preaching on John 3:7, "Ye must be born again.") After Liele's departure Bryan began to exhort blacks and whites. When he and a few followers started gathering in suburb of Savannah for worship, they were harassed by the white citizens, "as it was at a time when a number of blacks had absconded, and some had been taken away by the British." Andrew Bryan and his brother Sampson were hauled before the city magistrates for punishment. "These, with many others, were twice imprisoned, and about *fifty* were severely whipped, particularly *Andrew, who was cut, and bled abundantly.*" Reportedly, Andrew "told his persecutors that he rejoiced not only to be whipped, but would freely suffer death for the cause of Jesus Christ." Finally, the parallels to the Acts of the Apostles must have become too embarrassing to local officials, who examined and released them with permission to resume their worship, but only between sunrise and sunset. Andrew's master permitted the congregation to use his barn near Brampton, three miles outside of town, as a meeting place. In 1788 the white Baptist minister, Abraham Marshall, examined and baptized about forty people, and licensed Andrew to preach. After his master's death, Andrew obtained his freedom. . . .

In 1790 Bryan's church numbered 225 full communicants and about 350 converts, "many of whom" did not have their masters' permission to be baptized. By 1800 Bryan was able to inform Rippon that his church was no longer persecuted by men "in the presence, and with the approbation and encouragement of many of the white people."

173

## 6. ISAAC, A SLAVE PREACHER

Moses Grandy reported that his brother-in-law Isaac, a slave preacher, "was flogged, and his back pickled" for preaching at a clandestine service in the woods. His listeners were flogged and "forced to tell who else was there." Grandy claimed that slaves were often flogged "if they are found singing or praying at home." Despite the danger, slaves continued to hold their own religious gatherings because, as Grandy stated, "they like their own meetings better."

(Albert J. Raboteau, *Slave Religion* [Oxford University Press, 1978], p. 214. Source: Moses Grandy, *Narrative of the Life of Moses Grandy*, 2nd ed. [Boston, 1844], pp. 35-36.)

## 7. JAMES SMITH, A SLAVE PREACHER

Fugitive slave James Smith, while still enslaved in Virginia, joined the Baptist Church and felt a call to preach to his fellow slaves. To prevent him from preaching, his master kept him tied up all day on Sundays and, when he proved intransigent, flogged him as well. Nevertheless, Smith kept up his ministry as best he could and later reported that "many were led to embrace the Saviour under his preaching."

(Albert J. Raboteau, *Slave Religion*, p. 307.)

## 8. and 9. JOSEPH, JUDY HALFEN'S MOTHER, AND OTHERS

"One night Joe an' my mammy an' some more slaves wus down on deir knees prayin' fur de good Lord to sot dem free, an' Frances wus slippin' round de corner uf de house an' heard what dey wus sayin'. An' she goes back to de house an' tells de old marster, an' he sent de oberseer down dar an' brung ebery one uf dem to de stake, an' tied dem, an' whupped dem so hard dat blood come from some uf dem's backs."

(Judy Halfen. From *Bullwhip Days: The Slaves Remember,* James Mellon, ed. [New York, Avon Books, 1988], p. 196.)

## 10. THOMAS JONES

When Thomas Jones grew concerned about the state of his soul, his master told him to stop moping about, forbade him to attend prayer meetings, and ordered him to stop praying. In spite of repeated and severe whippings, Jones persisted in attending Methodist class meetings and refused to promise that he would abandon prayer.

(Albert J. Raboteau, *Slave Religion*, p. 307. Source: Thomas Jones,

*Narrative of a Refugee Slave: The Experience of Thomas Jones* [Springfield, Mass., 1854], pp. 20-27.)

## 11. AN ANONYMOUS SLAVE FROM COLUMBUS, KENTUCKY

"When I was a slave my master would sometimes whip me *awful,* specially when he knew I was praying. He was determined to whip the Spirit out of me, but he could never do it, for de more he whip the more the Spirit make me *content* to be whipt."

(From an interview conducted in Columbus, Kentucky by a white missionary from the North and published in *American Missionary,* February, 1863.)

## 12. REVEREND R. S. SORICK

Rev. R. S. Sorick, a slave preacher from Washington County, Maryland, was placed in prison in 1841 for three months and eight days "for preaching the gospel to my colored brethren."

(Benjamin Drew, *The Refugee: A North-Side View of Slavery* [Boston, 1856], p. 83.)

## 13. GUS CLARK

Gus Clark reported: "My Boss didn' 'low us to go to church, er to pray er sing. Iffen he ketched us prayin' er singin' he whupped us. . . . He didn' care fer nothin' 'cept farmin'."

(Albert J. Raboteau, *Slave Religion,* p. 214.)

## B. Those Who Confessed Christ Under Threat of Torture and Death

## 14. PRAYING JACOB

Praying Jacob was a slave in the state of Maryland. His master was very cruel to slaves. Jacob's rule was to pray three times a day, at just such an hour of the day; no matter what his work was or where he might be, he would stop and go and pray. His master has been to him and pointed his gun at him, and told him if he did not cease praying he would blow out his brains. Jacob would finish his prayer and tell his master to shoot in welcom—your loss will be my gain—I have two masters, one on earth and one in heaven—Master Jesus in heaven, and master Saunders on earth. I have a soul and a body; the body belongs to you, master Saunders, and the soul to Jesus. Jesus says men ought always to pray, but you will not pray, neither do you want to have me pray. . . .

Sometimes Mr. Saunders would be in the field about half drunk, raging like a madman, whipping the other slaves; and when Jacob's hour would come for prayer, he would . . . kneel down and pray, but he [Saunders] could not strike the man of God.

(G. W. Offley, *A Narrative of the Life and Labors of Rev. G. W. Offley* [Hartford, Connecticut, 1860], reprinted in *Five Black Lives,* pp. 134-135.)

## 15. ELI JOHNSON

Eli Johnson claimed that when he was threatened with five hundred lashes for holding prayer meetings, he stood up to his master and declared, "In the name of God why is it, that I can't after working hard all the week, have a meeting of Saturday evening? I'll suffer the flesh to be dragged off my bones . . . for the sake of my blessed Redeemer."

(Albert J. Raboteau, *Slave Religion,* p. 307. Source: Benjamin Drew, *The Refugee: A North-Side View of Slavery,* pp. 269-270.)

## 16. STEPHEN WILLIAMS' MOTHER

"I rec'lec' . . . [one night] the colored folks in the trader yard hold a prayer meeting. Mama was very religious—very religious—and if ever a soul went to Heaven, hers did. Seems like Major Long was gone that evening, and Mama and some more of the folks in the yard got together for a praying time. Didn' do no singin, 'cause that would have 'tracted attention, and the major didn't 'low no meetings. But someone saw the folks praying and told him the next morning, and he comes out in the yard with a cat-o'-nine-tails and rounds everybody up. Then, he said, 'You niggers what was praying last night, step out here.'

"None come out, though, 'cept Mama, 'cause they was 'fraid they was going to get whipped. Major said to Mama, 'Well, you are the only truthful one in the yard, and I won't whip you, 'cause you have been truthful.' . . . Mama jes' fell on her knees and thanked the good Lord right in front of the major, and he never touched her with the whip."

(Stephen Williams. From *Bullwhip Days.*)

*Special thanks to Michael Hatlin for helping us to find the original sources for this Martyrology.*

# APPENDIX II

# AKATHIST TO
# OUR HOLY FATHER
# AMONG THE SAINTS,
# MOSES THE BLACK

### *Kontakion 1*

Mighty ancient desert dweller of the Egyptian Thebaid, thy life is an everlasting memorial of the reconciliation between God and man. In thee we see the fullness of the fruits of repentance. Guide our steps onto the path of salvation as we call on thy all powerful prayer.

> Rejoice, holy elder Moses, righteous teacher of true spiritual wisdom!

### *Ikos 1*

In the days of thy youth, as a gang-leader thou was a ravenous wolf slaying sheep and murdering men. Yet in a moment of truth, God acted invisibly on thy conscience as thou was about to commit a crime, opening the door to the Way, the Truth and the Life. Following thy path toward the Light we sing these praises:

> Rejoice, model of correction for those who have gone astray.
>
> Rejoice, thou who didst die to earthly pleasures and resurrect in spirit.
>
> Rejoice, thou who camest out of much tribulation.
>
> Rejoice, oasis of faith in the desert of unbelief.

Rejoice, ancient treasure map for those seeking the pearl of great price.

Rejoice, for thou didst find the Kingdom of God within thy heart.

Rejoice, holy Elder Moses, righteous teacher of true spiritual wisdom!

## Kontakion 2

En route to great stature in grace, thou didst travel the path of lowliness, seeking counsel in all matters concerning spiritual life. Burying the instructions of the Fathers deep within thy heart thou didst always sing to God: Alleluia!

## Ikos 2

As thou didst possess self-knowledge and then ascend to wisdom on high, many seekers came to thee for spiritual guidance. With a pure mind thou didst teach in simplicity, revealing hidden truths to all who would listen. Help us now to understand and do God's will in our lives as we call upon thee:

Rejoice, thou who taughtest with power and not empty words.

Rejoice, for thy mind was renewed by prayer of the heart.

Rejoice, island of refuge for those sinking in the sea of temptation.

Rejoice, wellspring gushing forth with the words of life.

Rejoice, for the house of thy soul was not built on the sand of worldly knowledge but on the rock of Christ's commandments.

Rejoice, holy Elder Moses, righteous teacher of true spiritual wisdom.

## Kontakion 3

A brother came to thee for a word of instruction and in thy wisdom thou didst reveal the mystery of silence by saying, "Go to thy cell and thy cell will teach thee everything." Marveling at thy insight we raise up our minds unto God singing: Alleluia!

## Ikos 3

Through fire and water didst thou pass in thy struggle to conquer the lusts of the body. In thy quest, thou didst war against nature itself, depriving thy body of food and sleep. By spending the nights hauling water for the brethren thou didst prepare thy soul to become a habituation for the spirit. Yet still being tormented by this passion, thou was forced to call upon God for deliverance. Seeing thy thirst, the Lord has brought thee into a place of everlasting refreshment. Through thee we have learned to rely on God and not ourselves, and so we praise thee:

Rejoice, victorious conqueror in the war against the passions.

Rejoice, general in Christ's army.

Rejoice, valorous spirit in battle.

Rejoice, beacon of the light overcoming the principalities and powers of darkness.

Rejoice, thou who was made strong by surrendering thy weakness to God.

Rejoice, for the arrows of the enemy cannot touch thee.

Rejoice, holy elder Moses, righteous teacher of true spiritual wisdom.

### Kontakion 4

Amazed by the conversion of thy life and even yet more in awe of thy spiritual ascent, we see that truly all things are possible with God. Not lingering on the surface of newly found Orthodox faith, thou didst dive into the depths of apostolic Christianity. So now inspire us to enter into the heart of hearts, sensing the Kingdom within as we cry to God: Alleluia!

### Ikos 4

In fleeing the vanity of the world, thou didst desire to live in obscurity so as to be free from the glory of men. But as a city set on a hill cannot be hid, so too the splendor of thy virtue could not be concealed. Thou didst try to hide thy identity by telling those who sought "the great Moses" that he was a man of depraved character. By reviling thyself thou didst escape the trap of vainglory, but when the wisdom of the humility was found out, all glorified thy Father in heaven and now we praise thee:

Rejoice, thou who didst crucify thy flesh to become poor in spirit.

Rejoice, thou who didst find joy through mourning.

Rejoice, Israelite who didst see God in the purity of thy heart.

Rejoice, thou who art filled with everlasting righteousness.

Rejoice, thou who was reviled yet kept silence for Christ's sake.

Rejoice, and be glad for great is thy reward in heaven.

Rejoice, holy elder Moses, righteous teacher of true spiritual wisdom!

### Kontakion 5

O Moses, thou didst travel from the kingdom of Ethiopia to the land of Egypt in order to slay the spiritual Pharaoh. Now free from the bondage of the oppressor, thou dost chant eternal praise to God: Alleluia!

### Ikos 5

Behold all you who seek God, a new Moses has appeared in Egypt liberating those who were shackled in mental slavery and leading them into the promised land of faith, hope and love. Free in spirit we sing these praises:
Rejoice, thou who didst climb the mountain of God.
Rejoice, thou who was transfigured by the light of Christ.
Rejoice, chosen by God to be a leader of the people.
Rejoice, thou who didst pass over the sea of temptation dry shod.
Rejoice, deliverer of souls down pressed by sin.
Rejoice, holy Elder Moses, righteous teacher of true spiritual wisdom!

### Kontakion 6

When the counsel of monks gathered together to judge a brother who had transgressed, thou didst teach all by carrying a leaky bag of sand into the midst of the fathers, saying, "The sands are my sins running down behind me which I cannot even see, and yet I have come to judge another." In this wise, thou didst teach all the path of self-reproach and humility. Marveling at the wisdom given thee, we chant to God: Alleluia!

### Ikos 6

Unbeknownst to thee, thy words would be a testament of desert wisdom even unto this day. Together with all those monks who, throughout the ages have been guided aright by thy words, we cry out to thee:
Rejoice, counselor of divine intellect.
Rejoice, forefather of philokalic wisdom.
Rejoice, ancient mystic.
Rejoice, thou whose mind's eye was opened by grace.
Rejoice, seer of spiritual reality.
Rejoice, holy elder Moses, righteous teacher of true spiritual wisdom!

### Kontakion 7

Seeing the power of the Holy Spirit dwelling in thee, thy former gang members were also led to thoughts concerning the meaning of life, death and the path of salvation. Convicted by the purity of thy life, they too changed their evil ways and followed thee, learning to cry out to God: Alleluia!

### Ikos 7

Once a thief and a robber but now a good shepherd, thou art even at this moment calling lost sheep back to the straight and narrow way that leads to everlasting life. Pray that our hardened hearts and our darkened minds take heed to thy call as we sing these praises:

Rejoice, perfection of renunciation.

Rejoice, guide of all who struggle to put off the old man and be clothed in Christ.

Rejoice, good seed that brought forth fruit an hundred fold.

Rejoice, thou who through remembrance of death didst attain unto life.

Rejoice, thou who didst pass through the valley of the shadow of death.

Rejoice, for thy soul did find rest in the still waters of Christ.

Rejoice, holy elder Moses, righteous teacher of true spiritual wisdom!

### Kontakion 8

As a true rebel against the spirit of the world, thou didst leave off all attachment to temporal things, forsake thy past life like a dream, and flee to the utter desert to be alone with God. Admiring thy courage we glorify God: Alleluia!

### Ikos 8

Unaware of thy physical strength, a band of thieves foolishly tried to rob thy cell of earthly treasure that did not exist. Never missing a chance to save a soul, thou didst tie them up and drag them into church. In truth, thou didst take the Kingdom unto thy brother by force, showing him the power of faith. Marveling at thy mighty works we praise thee:

Rejoice, solid foundation of brotherly love.

Rejoice, thou who didst take no thought for food and raiment.

Rejoice, thou who didst follow the way of the cross by daily struggles.

Rejoice, thou who went from strength to strength to reach the Kingdom.

Rejoice, courageous soul that didst conquer fear by perfect love.

Rejoice, thou who ever abidest in God.

Rejoice, holy Elder Moses, righteous teacher of true spiritual wisdom!

### Kontakion 10

Wishing to save the world, the Saviour of all has sent a brilliant star to shine upon those lost in darkness. Seeing thy life as a light in the night, teaching, enlightening, and guiding us, we cry out to God: Alleluia!

### Ikos 10

Thou art a saving hand, O Father Moses, pulling up all who are drowning in a world of hate and confusion. Reaching out to thee, we ask for guidance in this life of trials and temptations. Ever hoping in God's mercy we cry out in faith:

Rejoice, uplifter of the downtrodden.

Rejoice, guardian of the soul in despair.

Rejoice, consolation of those who weep.

Rejoice, calm harbor for those tossed on the waves of this life.

Rejoice, redemptive sufferer.

Rejoice, thou who dost lead us to seek the peace that surpasses all understanding.

Rejoice, holy elder Moses, righteous teacher of true spiritual wisdom!

### Kontakion 11

As a co-struggler with the great Arsenius, thou didst share a bond of unity in the monastic mystery. While Arsenius practiced silence, thou didst exercise charity, sacrificing quietude to receive weary pilgrims with hospitality. With love thou didst feed many hungry souls, giving them strength to sing: Alleluia!

### Ikos 11

True to the vision of the Elder who saw great boats on the river, in the one was Arsenius with the Spirit of God traveling in silence, and thou was sailing in the other, accompanied by the angels and feeding a monk with sweet honey from the honeycomb. As recipients of thy lovingkindness we give thanks to thee thus:

Rejoice, warm heart of tender mercy.

Rejoice, thou who didst crucify thyself but show indulgence towards others.

Rejoice, thou who didst lay down thy life for thy brother.

Rejoice, river flowing into the sea of compassion.

Rejoice, thou whose Christianity was formed in the heart and manifest in deed.

Rejoice, thou who didst accept strangers as Christ Himself.

Rejoice, holy elder Moses, righteous teacher of true spiritual wisdom!

### Kontakion 12

Timeless preacher of repentance for all who find themselves astray from God's love, thou didst give hope to the hopeless reminding us that there is no sin that exceeds God's mercy. Moved to compunction, we offer our tears and sacrifice our broken hearts crying out from the depths of our souls to God: Alleluia!

### Ikos 12

Now swelling in the heavenly Zion, thou dost partake in the majestic glory of the Almighty. By thine all-powerful prayers, beseech Him to grant us the strength to overcome the temptations of sin and send down upon us peace and great mercy as we sing these praises:

Rejoice, thou who didst overcome the world.

Rejoice, flaming fire ablaze with the love of God.

Rejoice, guiding star of wise men.

Rejoice, thou who was lifted up on the wings of the Spirit.

Rejoice, thou who didst fly away to the heavenly homeland.

Rejoice, thou who art dwelling in the bosom of Abraham.

Rejoice, holy Elder Moses, righteous teacher of true spiritual wisdom!

### Kontakion 13

O holy and righteous elder Moses, brilliant sun shining down rays of hope upon a world eclipsed in darkness: Hear our supplication that we offer unto thee; help us who seek God's truth to be steadfast in fulfilling Christ's commandments, and save from the pit of Gehenna all who cry to God: Alleluia! (*repeat 3 times*)

*Repeat Ikos 1 and Kontakion 1.*

## Prayer to St. Moses

Thou didst forsake temporal riches, earthly fame, and fleshly pleasure and didst freely choose a life of poverty and deprivation to become rich in spirit. Having tasted the momentary sweetness of sin, thou didst foresee the bitter end that awaits a life of self-indulgence. Having stained thy hands with the blood of thy brother, thou didst foretaste the anguish of hell. From this pit, thou didst cry out to God Who raised thee up as a testimony of His almighty power. In thy ascent to near the Living God thou didst not spare thyself but willfully endured a life of hardship and struggle. By following the path of the Cross, thy soul was empowered by the might of the Holy Spirit, thy mind was illumined with the understanding of things divine, and thy heart was filled with the burning love of God for thy fellow man. And though thou didst live in ancient times and in a distant land, today we find ourselves faced with the same struggle to overcome the evil that lies within us. In these perilous times, we call on thy prayers—help us! For our brothers and sisters are dying daily and our children are born hopeless in a world barren of Christian love. Amidst these trials, we waver because our faith is weak and we know not how to endure suffering courageously. Pray that we be strengthened to live uprightly, walking in the light of the holy Gospel, ever seeking to do the will of God. And in the dreadful day of judgment, pray that we may be received with His Unoriginate Son, and His most holy and life creating Spirit, to whom belongs all glory, honour and worship, now and ever and to the ages of ages. Amen.

# APPENDIX III

# FURTHER
# INFORMATION

**Brotherhood of St. Moses the Black**
Fr. Moses Berry
4000 Cleveland Avenue
St. Louis, Missouri 63110
(314) 772-6609

For sales of An Unbroken Circle:
   Brotherhood of St. Moses the Black
   PO Box 63377
   St. Louis, Missouri 63163

**Ancient Christianity and African-America Conferences**
c/o Reconciliation Ministries/St. Mary of Egypt Orthodox Church
Fr. Paisius and Michaela Altschul
3101 Troost
Kansas City, Missouri 64109
(816) 931-4751

**Holy Resurrection Cemetery, Ash Grove, Missouri**
c/o Fr. Moses Berry
4000 Cleveland Avenue
St. Louis, Missouri 63110
(314) 772-6609

**St. Andrew Rublev Iconography School**
For information about commissioning icons, icon-painting instruction and lectures, contact:
Nun Catherine Weston
1901 N. Pennsylvania
Indianapolis, Indiana 46202-1417

"The Unchained Heart," a collection of fifteen spirituals performed by a Conference participant, is available from Heavenly Realm Tapes and CDs, 252 East 4th Street, Chico, California 95927.

# APPENDIX IV

# AN INVITATION

*Your responses to the following questions would be greatly appreciated. Please forward to: Brotherhood of St. Moses the Black, PO Box 63377, St. Louis, Missouri 63163. Anonymous replies are welcome.*

1. How did you hear about AN UNBROKEN CIRCLE?

2. How was it useful to you, personally and/or professionally?

3. What changes in format or content would you suggest to improve it?

# NOTES

1. Benedicta Ward, SLG, trans., *The Sayings of the Desert Fathers* (London: Mowbray & Co. LTD and Kalamazoo: Cistercian Publications, 1975).

2. Fathers Seraphim Rose and Herman Podmoshensky, eds., *The Northern Thebaid: Monastic Saints of the Russian North* (Platina, Calif.: St. Herman of Alaska Brotherhood, 1975).

3. G. E. H. Palmer, Philip Sherrard, Kallistos Ware, trans., *Philokalia*, vol. I (Boston, Mass.: Faber and Faber, 1988), p. 95.

4. Roy J. Defarrar, trans., *St. Basil: The Letters*, vol. III (Cambridge, Mass.: Harvard University Press, 1962), p. 185.

5. John Heston Willey, *Chrysostom: The Orator* (Cincinnati, Ohio: Jennings and Graham, 1906), p. 58.

6. Metropolitan Anastassy, *A Defense of Monasticism* (Jordanville, N.Y.: Holy Trinity Monastery, 1989), p. 32.

7. I. M. Kontzevitch, *The Acquisition of the Holy Spirit in Ancient Russia* (Platina, Calif.: St. Herman of Alaska Brotherhood, 1988), p. 96.

8. St. Augustine, *Confessions* (trans. Dr. E. B. Pusey; New York: E. P. Dutton & Co., Inc., 1951), chapters 14 and 15.

9. Ibid., chapter 29.

10. Phillip Schaff, ed., *Nicene & Post Nicene Fathers*, 2nd series, vol. 3 (Peabody, Mass.: Hendrickson Publishers, 1994), p. 379.

11. Ibid., vol. 6, p. 38.

12. Ibid., p. 255.

13. Ibid., vol. 3, pp. 387-396.

14. St. Gregory of Tours, *Vita Patrum: The Life of the Fathers,* ed. Fr. Seraphim Rose (Platina, Calif.: St. Herman of Alaska Brotherhood, 1988).
15. Ibid., pp. 18-19.
16. Anthony C. Meisel and M. L. del Mastro, trans., *The Rule of St. Benedict* (New York: Doubleday, 1975), pp. 18-19.
17. St. Gregory of Tours, *Vita Patrum,* p. 95.
18. Ibid., p. 104.
19. Ibid., p. 99.
20. Edward C. Sellner, *Wisdom of the Celtic Saints* (Notre Dame, Ind.: Ave Maria Press, 1993), pp. 182-183.
21. Venerable Bede, *Life of Cuthbert* (trans. J. F. Webb; New York: Viking Penguin Books, 1988), pp. 68-69.
22. Kontzevitch, p. 99.
23. Saints Barsanuphius and John, *Guidance Toward Spiritual Life: Answers to the Questions of Disciples* (trans. Fr. Seraphim Rose; Platina, Calif.: St. Herman of Alaska Brotherhood, 1990).
24. Kontzevitch, p.108.
25. E. A. Wallis Budge, trans., *Paradise of the Holy Fathers* (Seattle, Wash.: St. Nectarios Press, 1984).
26. Kontzevitch, p. 98.
27. G. E. H. Palmer, Philip Sherrard, and Kallistos Ware, trans., *Philokalia,* vol. I, p. 12.
28. Kontzevitch, p. 169.
29. Ibid.
30. Ibid., pp. 170-171.
31. St. Macarius the Great, *Fifty Spiritual Homilies* (trans. A. J. Mason; Willits, Calif.: Eastern Orthodox Books, 1991), p. 89.
32. Leo the Great, Bishop of Rome, *The Sermons of Leo the Great* (trans. Rev. Charles Feltoe), vol. 12, *Nicene and Post Nicene Fathers,* ed. Philip Schaff (Peabody, Mass.: Hendrickson Pub., 1994), p. 204.
33. Bishop Nikolai Velimirovich, *The Prologue from Ochrid,* vol. 4 (Birmingham, England: Lazarica Press, 1986), p. 335.
34. Met. Anthony Khrapovitsky, "Christ the Savior and the Jewish Revolution" (comp. Fr. Demetrios Serfes; trans. Isaac Lambertsen), *Orthodox Life,* vol. 35, no. 4, July-Aug., pp. 11-31.
35. Velimirovitch, p. 335.
36. See Lorenzo Scupoli, *Unseen Warfare,* ed. Nicodemus of the Holy Mountain (rev. Bp. Theophan the Recluse; trans. E. Kadloubovsky and G. E. H. Palmer; Crestwood, N.Y.: St. Vladimir's Seminary Press, 1978), p. 81.
37. Johanna Manley, ed., *Grace for Grace: The Psalter and the Holy Fathers* (Menlo Park, Calif.: Monastery Books, 1992), pp. 551-553. Source: Blessed Augustine of Hippo, *On the Psalms* (1,2,3,4), *The Nicene and Post Nicene Fathers,* first series, vol. VIII (Grand Rapids: Wm. B. Eerdmans Pub., 1978), pp. 616-617.
38. Ibid.

39. *Paradise of the Holy Fathers,* vol. I (trans. E. A. Wallis Budge; Seattle, Wash.: St. Nectarios Press, 1984), pp. 127-128.

40. The tablets of the ten commandments that are kept in the Holy of Holies of each church, representing the submission of the people to God's will and law.

41. Aster Bekele, conversation with author, 31 January 1996; *New York Times,* 4-8 March 1896; Graham Hancock, *The Sign and the Seal: the Quest for the Lost Ark of the Covenant* (New York: Crown Pub., 1992), p. 196; Michael Clodfelter, *Warfare and Armed Conflicts: A Statistical Reference to Casualty and Other Figures, 1618-1991,* vol. I (Jefferson, North Carolina: McFarland & Co., 1992), p. 345.

42. Fr. Asteraye Nigatu, "Ethiopia: Its Christian Culture" (address given at the Ancient Christianity Conference, Indianapolis, 10 January 1996).

43. "St. Menas, Great Martyr and Wonderworker of Egypt," *The Orthodox Word,* vol. 3, no. 4 (15) Aug.-Sept. 1967, pp. 125-126.

44. Hieromonk Damascene, discussion period following "The Challenge of Meekness" (Ancient Christianity Conference; see note 11, above).

45. Hieromonk Damascene and Lucille C. Gunning, M.D., discussion period following "The Challenge of Meekness" (Ancient Christianity Conference; see note 11, above).

46. *Nicene and Post Nicene Fathers,* vol. 12, p. 40.

47. *The Collected Works of Phillis Wheatley,* ed. John Shields (New York, Oxford: Oxford University Press, 1988).

48. Peter Kalm, *Travels Into North America,* 2nd ed., reprinted in vol. 13 of *A General Collection of the Best and Most Interesting Voyages and Travels,* ed. John Pinkerton (London, 1812), p. 503.

49. Appeal to Governor Thomas Gage and the Massachusetts General Court, May 25, 1774, *Collection of the Massachusetts Historical Society,* 5th series, 3 (1877): 432-33.

50. George P. Rawick, ed., *The American Slave: A Composite Autobiography,* vol. 8, *Arkansas Narratives* (Westport, Conn.: Greenwood Press, 1972), pt. 1, 35.

51. Benjamin Drew, *The Refugee: A North-Side View of Slavery* (Boston, 1856), p. 55.

52. Moses Grandy, *Narrative of the Life of Moses Grandy,* 2nd ed. (Boston, 1844), pp. 35-36; Rawick, 7, *Mississippi,* p. 24; Henry Bibb, *Narrative of the Life and Adventures of Henry Bibb* (New York, 1849), reprinted in *Puttin' On Ole Massa,* ed. Gilbert Osofsky (New York: Harper & Row, 1969), pp. 123-125.

53. John Rippon, *The Baptist Annual Register,* 1790-1793 (n.p., n.d.), pp. 340-341.

54. Drew, p. 270.

55. John Blassingame, ed., *Slave Testimony* (Baton Rouge: Louisiana State University Press, 1977), pp. 276-278.

56. Rawick, 6, *Indiana,* p. 159.

57. *American Missionary,* series 2, 11 (May 1862): 102.

58. Rawick, 17, *Florida,* p. 166.

59. Clifton H. Johnson, ed., *God Struck Me Dead: Religious Conversion Experiences and Autobiographies of Ex-Slaves* (Philadelphia: Pilgrim Press, 1969), p. 76.

60. Rawick, 4, *Texas,* pt. 1, p. 199.

61. David Macrae, *The Americans at Home,* 2 vols. (Edinburgh, 1870), 2:102.

62. Johnson, ed., *God Struck Me Dead,* p. 74.

63. *American Missionary,* series 2, 6 (June 1862): 138.

64. Frederick Douglass, *The Life and Times of Frederick Douglass* (rev. ed. 1892; London: Collier-Macmillan, 1962), p. 135.

65. Charles Carleton Coffin, *The Boys of '61; or Four Years of Fighting* (Boston, 1886), p. 415.

66. Barbara Leigh Smith Bodichon, diary entry of 12 December 1857, in *An American Diary, 1857-1858,* ed. Joseph W. Reed, Jr. (London: Routledge and Kegan Paul, 1972), p. 65.

67. See Johnson, ed., *God Struck Me Dead,* pp. 23, 78.

68. William Grimes, *Life of William Grimes* (New Haven, Conn.: 1855); reprinted in *Five Black Lives* (Middletown, Conn.: Wesleyan University Press, 1971), pp. 198-199.

69. Drew, p. 181.

70. Howard Thurman, *With Hand and Heart: The Autobiography of Howard Thurman* (New York: Harcourt, Brace, Jovanovich, 1979), p. 134.

71. SS. Barsanuphius and John, *Guidance Toward Spiritual Life* (Platina, Calif.: St. Herman of Alaska Brotherhood, 1990), p. 144.

72. St. Maximus the Confessor, *Selected Writings* (New York: Paulist Press, 1985), pp. 42, 51. Cf. Galatians 3:28 and Ephesians 1:23.

73. Richard Wurmbrand, *Tortured for Christ* (Glendale, Calif.: Diane Books, 1969), pp. 15-16.

74. Richard Wurmbrand, *In God's Underground* (New York: Bantam Books, 1968), p. 1.

75. Wurmbrand, *Tortured for Christ,* p. 39.

76. Ibid., pp. 45, 57.

77. Wurmbrand, *In God's Underground,* p. 100.

78. Fr. George Calciu, *Christ is Calling You!* (Platina, Calif.: St. Herman of Alaska Brotherhood, 1997), pp. 135-137.

79. Ibid., p. 118.

80. Ibid., pp. 137-138.

81. I. M. Andreyev, *Russian Catacomb Saints* (Platina, Calif.: St. Herman of Alaska Brotherhood, 1982), pp. 412-413.

82. Peter Randolph, *Slave Cabin to Pulpit* (Boston, 1893).

83. James Mellon, ed., *Bullwhip Days: The Slaves Remember, An Oral History* (New York: Avon Books, 1988).

84. Albert J. Raboteau, *Slave Religion: The "Invisible Institution" in the Antebellum South* (New York: Oxford University Press, 1978), p. 217.

85. Ibid., pp. 227-228.

86. Ibid., p. 270.

87. Dwight D. Hopkins and George C. L. Cummings, eds., *Cut Loose Your Stammering Tongue: Black Theology in the Slave Narratives* (Maryknoll, New York: Orbis Books, 1991), pp. 25-26.

88. Ibid.

89. Raboteau, p. 302.

90. Marion Wilson Starling, ed., *The Slave Narrative: Its Place in American History* (Washington, D.C.: Howard University Press, 1988), p. 117.

91. Raboteau, p. 308.

92. Ibid., p. 306.

93. St. Dorotheus of Gaza, *Discourses and Sayings* (Kalamazoo, Michigan: Cistercian Publications, 1977), p. 96.

94. John F. Bayliss, *Black Slaves Narratives* (New York: Macmillan, 1970), p. 122.

95. Ibid., pp. 130-132.

96. Raboteau, p. 292.

97. Ibid., pp. 213-214.

98. Randolph, *Slave Cabin to Pulpit.*

99. St. Maximus the Confessor, quoted in Vladimir Lossky, *The Mystical Theology of the Eastern Church* (Cambridge: James Clarke & Co., 1957).

100. Starling, ed., *The Slave Narratives*, pp. 161-162.

101. Raboteau, p. 237.

102. Ibid., p. 242.

103. Ibid., p. 267.

104. James Weldon Johnson, *The Book of American Negro Spirituals* (New York: Viking Press, 1925), pp. 12-13.

105. Ibid., p. 11.

106. John and Alan Lomax, *101 American Folk Songs.*

107. Federal Writers Project. Tom Robinson, age 88, Catamba County, North Carolina. Interviewed by Mary P. Hudgins.

108. Raboteau, pp. 310-311.

109. Ibid., p. 315.

110. Mellon, ed., *Bullwhip Days.*

111. Raboteau, p. 308.

112. Ibid., p. 309.

113. Ibid., p. 308.

114. Jeff Jacoby, "Christian Suffering is on the Rise," *Boston Globe*, December 4, 1996, p. A15.

115. For a free subscription to the *Voice of the Martyrs Newsletter,* book and video information, and ways to help suffering Christians, contact: The Voice of the Martyrs, PO Box 443, Bartlesville, OK 74005, (918)337-8015.

116. Larry Elevtherios Johnson, "Trust in God . . . and Forgive," *Again,* vol. 17, no. 2, June 1994, p. 9.

117. Federal Writers Project. Doc Daniel Dowdy, age 81, Oklahoma City, Oklahoma. Formerly a slave in Georgia.

118. Bayliss, *Black Slaves Narratives,* pp. 86-90.

119. Rev. Jesse Lee Peterson, "Black Mind Control," *B.O.N.D. Newsletter,* Jan.-Feb., 1997. Contact B.O.N.D., PO Box 86253, Los Angeles, CA 90086-0253, 800-411-BOND). Also contact Edmund Peterson, Chairman of Project 21, 300 I St. NE, Suite 3, Washington, DC 20002.

120. Archimandrite Panteleimon, comp., *A Ray of Light: Instructions in Piety and the State of the World at the End of Time* (Jordanville, N.Y.: Holy Trinity Monastery, 1991), p. 80.

121. Gennady Durasov, *Beloved Sufferer: The Life and Mystical Revelations of a Russian Eldress, Schemanun Macaria* (Platina, Calif.: St. Herman of Alaska Brotherhood, 1995).

122. Fathers Seraphim Rose and Herman Podmoshensky, eds., *The Northern Thebaid: Monastic Saints of the Russian North* (Platina, Calif.: St. Herman of Alaska Brotherhood, 1975).

123. Prayer Book (Jordanville, N.Y.: Holy Trinity Monastery).